THE OFFICIAL'S ROLE IN IMPROVING SPORTSMANSHIP

Edited by Jim Arehart, *Referee* senior managing editor

From *Referee* Magazine and the National Association of Sports Officials

The Official's Role in Improving Sportsmanship
Edited by Jim Arehart, *Referee* senior managing editor
Cover and layout by Rob VanKammen, *Referee* graphic designer

Copyright © 2005
Reprinted 2006
by *Referee* Enterprises, Inc.
P.O. Box 161, Franksville, Wis. 53126.

Printed in the United States of America

ISBN 1-58208-058-5

Table of Contents

The NASO Sports Officiating 2004 Summit, with the theme of "The Official's Role in Improving Sportsmanship," served as the basis for this book, supplemented by material published in *Referee* magazine and a variety of NASO publications, as well as information gathered from previous NASO Summits.

INTRODUCTION

When a 2004 NASO survey asked 550 sports officials what they thought the number-one problem is in our games today, it's probably not too surprising that the resounding answer was poor sportsmanship.

After all, it was only a few years ago that surveys by both NASO and the NFHS indicated that poor behavior on the part of spectators, players and coaches was the biggest force driving men and women out of the officiating ranks.

NASO brought together some of the best and the brightest in youth, high school, collegiate and pro sports from Aug. 7-9, 2004, to examine the issue of sportsmanship and the official's role in promoting positive onfield behavior.

Since 2000, NASO's annual gathering has focused on an area of concern directly affecting the world of officiating. Previous topics have been recruiting and retention of officials, defining officiating excellence, methods of training and accountability of officials.

This year's Summit on sportsmanship drew more than 300 attendees, including 25 state association administrators from 20 different states. "I am sure there were a variety of motives for the various state office people to attend," said attendee and session panelist Ralph Swearngin, executive director of the Georgia High School Association. "I believe that the focus on sportsmanship was the bridge to bring state associations to an officiating conference. I also believe that NASO has been initiating more contacts with state associations and their personnel, and that is proving to be productive for everyone."

For the past several years, the NFHS has partnered with NASO in producing the Summit.

"The state associations and NFHS understand that officials play a major role in sponsoring wholesome activities for our students," said attendee Larry Thomas, associate director of the Mississippi High School Athletic Association. "The NFHS's promotion of the NASO Summit helped provide an avenue for the state association to secure information to make the game better and form a better relationship with the officials."

"Civility is almost a lost art in our society today," said Bob Kanaby, NFHS executive director, during the session "View From the Top." "People just aren't civil to each other. People are afraid to say hello or good morning to each other. You get in an elevator with another individual and nobody says anything. Will (civility) ever swing back to the good old days? Frankly, the good old days, weren't that good when you start to look at them. I heard a great comment about it: 'If you spend all your time trying to recreate the good old days, then you lose the todays and the tomorrows.'"

That's why attendees at the D.C. Summit focused their energies on ways to become part of the solution here and now.

The sportsmanship theme was just one draw. The fact that the NASO Summit draws officiating leaders from hundreds of local associations, national organizations and youth leagues, as well as college and professional officiating groups, means that officiating discussions at the Summit permeate the entire scope of athletics in the country.

"Officiating is certainly a priority at the national level and the leadership there shows that," said attendee Tom Robinson, Colorado High School Activities Association (CHSAA) assistant commissioner. "I know that (CHSAA) Commissioner Bill Reader has made it a priority for our association, and NASO is definitely a conference I will always attend."

1

The Sportsmanship Puzzle

In this chapter ...

- **Root Causes of Poor Sportsmanship**
  Why it's a problem.

- **What is Good Sportsmanship?**
  Perspectives on positive behavior in sports.

- **How Officials Impact Sportsmanship**
  Where officials and the actions of officials influence the behaviors of players, coaches and spectators.

In his book, *What's Wrong With Sports,* Howard Cosell wrote, "There is a harsh truth in America today. Sports have become a great emotional outlet and escape for the country. To millions, involvement in the sports world is a fantasy-like experience in which the average American can forget his or her everyday troubles.

"Sports have become a necessity in the lives of the American people and the ramifications of this need threaten to invade every avenue of American life.

"It's no simple matter. Sport as we know it today involves labor laws, sociology and politics. The industry, amateur and professional, has become so greedy and massive that it has lost perspective and suffered a decline in values."

That was written 13 years ago and while much in sports has improved during that time, that loss of perspective likely has not. In fact, it is likely that in some measure things are more complicated, especially for officials.

A few years ago, people leaving the avocation of officiating was reaching epidemic proportions. Recruitment of new officials was stagnant and retention of existing officials was abysmal. In some areas of the country, we're starting to see some improvement in that area, but the need for officials in many other areas indicates we're still at a crisis with the overall population of officials.

It's been stated over and over again that the single biggest reason why new people don't join the officiating avocation and why existing officials leave the avocation has to do with the poor — often outrageous — behavior of others involved in sports, from players to coaches to parents and other spectators.

The issue of poor sportsmanship is important in officiating because it could impact the very survival of what officials do. How and why did we ever get to this point?

Root Causes of Poor Sportsmanship

Much has been written on why the state of sportsmanship in our sports is decaying. There are four popular theories that often make the rounds:

1. It's the pro athletes' fault. There's the "trickle-down" effect from the pro sports, where the antics of such "role models" as Randy Moss, Roger Clemens and Ron Artest are on full display. Kids watch their heroes behave poorly and think that's how it's done.

2. It's the parents' fault. There's the parent effect, whereby kids are allowed, sometimes even encouraged, to act in an inappropriate manner by parents who feel it's "part of the game" to yell at game officials, throw equipment or sulk about perceived bad calls or engage in such things as taunting or even cheating during the course of the game.

3. It's the coaches' fault. Ideally, athletes express physical skill and learn about competition, character and sportsmanship. All scholastic sports, after all, are an extension of the classroom. Effectively, that makes the coach the teacher. But how many other teachers are subject to the kinds of pressures as coaches are? Few local newspapers publish articles calling for the immediate firing of a high school's math teacher, for example. Coaches are under enormous pressure to deliver victories and as such, some coaches have been known too turn a blind eye to acts of poor sportsmanship — especially if addressing such behavior would be a detriment to winning.

4. It's society's fault. People often argue that sportsmanship is on the decline because basic civility in our society is on the decline. As NFHS Executive Director Bob Kanaby said, "Civility is almost a lost art in our society today."

Kanaby called for moving forward with solutions while learning from the past. "I don't ever remember anybody talking to me when I was growing up about being civil," he said. "But it was an expectation that somehow permeated me and I understood what they were talking about. The coaches who transmitted those things, the officials who transmitted those things, in some measure have gone by the wayside. We need to go back and reteach those things. We need to actually go back and say, 'Hey, we expect you to be civil. We expect you to be courteous.' They just don't happen automatically anymore. All of our organizations have realized that and through the rules and regulations of our games and programs that are positive in nature, we're trying to go back and reteach civility, sportsmanship and good behavior. Those are expectations and those are the things we have to do."

There are probably 100 more reasons you could point to for why we're seeing so much poor sportsmanship these days. It's most likely that there is no single identifiable cause for the decline in sportsmanship. More likely it's a complex combination of the previous four theories as well as 100 other reasons.

To understand how and why we're in the state we're in, we need to know where we'd like to be.

What is Good Sportsmanship?

Kids practice good sportsmanship when they treat their teammates, opponents, coaches and officials with respect. In practice, good sportsmanship often is about controlling one's own frustrations, while being courteous to all others involved in the sports experience. That extends beyond the onfield or oncourt participants to the coaches and other personnel on or near the bench. It also extends to spectators, whether it's a small gathering of parents at a Little League game or a huge crowd at a high school or college match.

Being respectful and courteous are great goals, but true sportsmanship is not just about being a nice person; it is much more important than that. It's about character.

Character is the core issue of sportsmanship, according to Michael Josephson, the founder and president of the Josephson Institute of Ethics. Josephson is also an NASO board member, and while speaking at the 2004 Summit, he explained his "Six

Pillars of Character." They are: trustworthiness, respect, responsibility, fairness, caring and citizenship. Josephson described the Six Pillars of Character as ethical values to guide our choices. The standards of conduct that arise out of those values constitute the ground rules of ethics, and therefore of ethical decision-making.

Josephson's institute founded the youth-oriented Character Counts! program to foster character in young people along with the "Pursuing Victory With Honor" program focusing specifically on athletics and sportsmanship.

As Josephson explained, the Six Pillars act as a multi-level filter through which to process decisions. For example, being trustworthy is not enough — we must also be caring. Adhering to the letter of the law is not enough — we must accept responsibility for our action or inaction, etc.

The Pillars can help us detect situations in which we focus so hard on upholding one moral principle that we sacrifice another — where, intent on holding others accountable, we ignore the duty to be compassionate; where, intent on getting a job done, we ignore how.

Josephson summarized the Pillars at the NASO Summit, based on the following outline:

THE SIX PILLARS OF CHARACTER
1. TRUSTWORTHINESS

When others trust us, they give us greater leeway because they feel we don't need monitoring to assure that we'll meet our obligations. They believe in us and hold us in higher esteem. That's satisfying. At the same time, we must constantly live up to the expectations of others and refrain from even small lies or self-serving behavior that can quickly destroy our relationships.

Simply refraining from deception is not enough. Trustworthiness is the most complicated of the six core ethical values and concerns a variety of qualities like honesty, integrity, reliability and loyalty.

Honesty — There is no more fundamental ethical value than honesty. We associate honesty with people of honor, and we admire and rely on those who are honest. But honesty is a broader concept than many may realize. It involves both communications and conduct. Honesty in communications is expressing the truth as best we know it and not conveying it in a way likely to mislead or deceive.

Integrity — The word integrity comes from the same Latin root as "integer," or whole number. Like a whole number, a person of integrity is undivided and complete. That means that the ethical person acts according to his or her beliefs, not according to expediency. Such people are also consistent. There is no difference in the way they make decisions from situation to situation, their principles don't vary at work or at home, in public or alone.

Reliability — When we make promises or other commitments that create a legitimate basis for another person to rely upon us, we undertake special moral duties. We accept the responsibility of making all reasonable efforts to fulfill our commitments.

Loyalty — Some relationships — husband-wife, employer-employee, citizen-country — create an expectation of allegiance, fidelity and devotion. Loyalty is a responsibility to promote the interests of certain people, organizations or affiliations. That duty goes beyond the normal obligation we all share to care for others.

2. RESPECT

People are not things, and everyone has a right to be treated with dignity. We certainly have no ethical duty to hold all people in high esteem, but we should treat everyone with respect, regardless of who they are and what they have done. We have a responsibility to be the best we can be in all situations, even when dealing with unpleasant people.

The Golden Rule — do unto others as you would have them do unto you — nicely illustrates the Pillar of respect. Respect prohibits violence, humiliation, manipulation and exploitation. It reflects notions such as civility, courtesy, decency, dignity, autonomy, tolerance and acceptance.

▶ **Civility, Courtesy and Decency** — A respectful person is an attentive listener, although his or her patience with the boorish need not be endless (respect works both ways). Nevertheless, the respectful person treats others with consideration, and doesn't resort to intimidation, coercion or violence except in extraordinary and limited situations to defend others, teach discipline, maintain order or achieve social justice. Punishment is used in moderation and only to advance important social goals and purposes.

▶ **Dignity and Autonomy** — People need to make informed decisions about their own lives. Don't withhold the information they need to do so. Allow all individuals, including maturing children, to have a say in the decisions that affect them.

▶ **Tolerance and Acceptance** — Accept individual differences and beliefs without prejudice. Judge others only on their character, abilities and conduct.

3. RESPONSIBILITY

Life is full of choices. Being responsible means being in charge of our choices and, thus, our lives. It means being accountable for what we do and who we are. It also means recognizing that our actions matter and we are morally on the hook for the consequences. Our capacity to reason and our freedom to choose make us morally autonomous and, therefore, answerable for whether we honor or degrade the ethical principles that give life meaning and purpose.

Ethical people show responsibility by being accountable, pursuing excellence and exercising self-restraint. They exhibit the ability to respond to expectations.

▶ **Accountability** — An accountable person is not a victim and doesn't shift blame or claim credit for the work of others. Such people consider the likely consequences of their behavior and associations. They recognize the common complicity in the triumph of evil when nothing is done to stop it. They lead by example.

▶ **Pursuit of Excellence** — The pursuit of excellence has an ethical dimension when others rely upon our knowledge, ability or willingness to perform tasks safely and effectively.

▶ **Self-Restraint** — Responsible people exercise self-control, restraining passions and appetites (such as lust, hatred, gluttony, greed and fear) for the sake of longer-term vision and better judgment. They delay gratification if necessary and never feel it's necessary to "win at any cost." They realize they are as they choose to be, every day.

4. FAIRNESS

What is fairness? Most would agree it involves issues of equality, impartiality, proportionality, openness and due process. Most would agree that it is unfair to handle similar matters inconsistently. Most would agree that it is unfair to impose punishment that is not commensurate with the offense. The basic concept seems simple, even intuitive, yet applying it in daily life can be surprisingly difficult. Fairness is another tricky concept, probably more subject to legitimate debate and interpretation than any other ethical value. Disagreeing parties tend to maintain that there is only one fair position (their own, naturally). But essentially fairness implies adherence to a balanced standard of justice without relevance to one's own feelings or inclinations.

▶ **Process** — Process is crucial in settling disputes, both to reach the fairest results and to minimize complaints. A fair person scrupulously employs open and impartial processes for gathering and evaluating information necessary to make decisions. Fair people do not wait for the truth to come to them; they seek out relevant information and conflicting perspectives before making important judgments.

▶ **Impartiality** — Decisions should be made without favoritism or prejudice.

▶ **Equity** — An individual, company or society should correct mistakes, promptly and voluntarily. It is improper to take advantage of the weakness or ignorance of others.

5. CARING

If you existed alone in the universe, there would be no need for ethics and your heart could be a cold, hard stone. Caring is the heart of ethics, and ethical decision-making. It is scarcely possible to be truly ethical and yet unconcerned with the welfare of others. That is because ethics is ultimately about good relations with other people.

It is easier to love "humanity" than to love people. People who consider themselves ethical and yet lack a caring attitude toward individuals tend to treat others as instruments of their will. They rarely feel an obligation to be honest, loyal, fair or respectful except insofar as it is prudent for them to do so, a disposition that itself hints at duplicity and a lack of integrity. A person who really cares feels an emotional response to both the pain and pleasure of others.

6. CITIZENSHIP

Citizenship includes civic virtues and duties that prescribe how we ought to behave as part of a community. The good citizen knows the laws and obeys them, volunteers and stays informed on the issues of the day, the better to execute his or her duties and privileges as a member of a self-governing democratic society. The good citizen does more than his or her "fair" share to make society work, now and for future generations. Such a commitment to the public sphere can have many expressions, such as conserving resources, recycling, using public transportation and cleaning up litter. The good citizen gives more than he or she takes.

Josephson's Six Pillars were written with young people in mind because young people are the most impressionable and are still forming their character. But the ideals expressed within those

Six Pillars are applicable to all segments of society, especially when it comes to sportsmanship.

We've taken a look at some of the root causes for poor sportsmanship and we've seen an ideal for how we'd like our athletes, coaches and spectators to behave, yet there's been no mention of officials. What is our role in solving the sportsmanship equation?

How Officials Impact Sportsmanship

As we'll learn in later chapters, we're not wholly outside of the issue of sportsmanship. We may be impartial observers, the middlemen and women who keep things fair, but we definitely have an impact on the behavior of others during any game. Sometimes we do it unknowingly, and other times we interject ourselves with full awareness that we're influencing the behavior of others.

The most obvious way officials influence the behavior of others during a game is simply by making calls. That's why officials are there, and the old cliché about only ever being able to please half the people at any given game is exactly right. Referees and umpires are not popular with participants and spectators no matter how good their officiating skills are, and they never will be. Making calls — unpopular or otherwise — is the function of sports officials.

The less obvious way officials influence the behavior of others during a game has nothing to do with making calls, but has everything to do with not making calls. Officials are responsible for fostering poor sportsmanship when they deliberately ignore or make allowances for actions and behavior that leads to a negative sporting experience.

It's a common scene in games these days: The official clearly warning a nearby coach or player that that's enough. Maybe he's putting up the "stop sign" with his hands. Maybe you can see him having a quiet word with the coach or player. But how effective are those warnings if there's never any follow through?

NASO President Barry Mano contended in the January 2004 issue of *Referee* magazine that referees, with society's nudging, are softening. They're beginning to view the best path to success as the one that avoids the most controversy. Mano called it the trend toward "the kinder, gentler official," and that's not a compliment. He's talking about the person who works a game but looks for every possible way to not be the bad guy — often to the detriment of the sport. When the situation calls for a "T," he lets a player off with a warning to behave. When a player grabs every shirt in sight, he tells him he'd better not do it again … and again … and again. This is the world of "next time" and many agree that it's as dangerous as it is make-believe.

Turning a blind eye to certain behaviors can cause big problems not only in that single game but also for every official that comes afterward and every season afterward until it becomes nearly impossible to go back to the way it should be.

If officials are tolerant of certain behaviors, those behaviors become ingrained and repeated. Here are four areas of concern that, if left unchecked by officials, could rapidly turn sports into a wasteland of poor behavior.

Taunting and Rough Play

Few game-related actions will set tempers flaring quicker than taunting and rough play. You can expect to see some sort of retaliation if one participant mocks or disrespects an opponent. Expect even quicker retaliation if one player swings an elbow extra hard in the direction of his or her opponent. Nobody likes to be roughed up and a natural human instinct is to lash out when suffering a blow.

Officials can stem those retaliations by stepping in immediately and penalizing such actions. That way, the aggressor is dealt some payback within the scope of the game and the victimized athlete can more easily disengage from the brewing conflict.

Officials who are inclined to mete out warnings for such behavior might think they are managing the game with a soft hand, but often that will only invite retaliation, which will escalate as the game progresses.

Rick Hartzell, a veteran of more than 1,600 NCAA Division I men's basketball games, wonders what our lives would be like if we handled our families the same way he sees some officials handling players.

"Suppose you're sitting having dinner and your son decides that it's a great idea to start throwing peas at his sister," he begins. "As he raises his arm, you say, 'Don't throw that pea at your sister,' and then he does anyway. Then, as he reloads, you warn him again and he does it again. After about the third time, he concludes that you aren't really serious. Then he wonders what else he can get away with."

Stop a Problem Before It Starts

☐ **Continue to officiate in dead-ball situations** — When the whistle blows, that's when trash talking can start. That can lead to a push or a shove and things can quickly slide downhill. If you have a held ball call, particularly if two players are scrambling on the floor, get close to the two individuals involved and let them know you're there. If they see your striped shirt, they'll generally get up and move away from each other. If you're the line judge and a runner is driven out of bounds along your sideline, don't worry about staying at the dead-ball spot. That's why you have a beanbag. Stay with the players. Again, just the fact that they know you're there can prevent problems.

☐ **Talk to your partners so that players can hear you** — Talking to your fellow officials in front of the players can head off an abundance of difficulties. If, for instance, two post players are jostling one another, at the next free-throw situation say something like, "Bill, keep an eye on 25 white and I'll watch 34 red." That lets the players know you're watching them. Use a normal conversational tone and don't stare down either player. You've gotten your message across in a non-threatening way.

☐ **Keep your eye on the ball** — That technique works particularly well in baseball. If a pitcher has been complaining about your strike zone, ask to see the ball. Wipe it off, or in fact actually change it, then walk about three quarters of the way to the mound and toss the pitcher the baseball. Then tell him in a normal voice that you've heard enough for one day. He'll get the message that, 1) you have indeed heard enough and, 2) that you're doing your best to keep him in the game.

The solution, says Hartzell, is not to worry about being friends with your children any more than being friends with the players when trouble's brewing. "What you'd do with your son," Hartzell goes on, "is tell him the first time he takes aim, 'If you throw the pea, you're going to your room.' Then, if he does, it's *whack*, 'Go to your room.' There's no middle ground. 'I told you what would happen and you did it anyway. Goodbye.' He's had his chance. Then, when he's sitting in his room wishing he could be back at the table eating and doing all that other fun stuff, he gets the idea not to try that again. And probably nobody else at the table will try either because they've seen what will happen."

Cheating and Gamesmanship

If cheating — or its close relative (and oftentimes identical twin) gamesmanship — is part of the game, nobody told the folks who write the rules. Take a look at any rulebook at any level and, contrary to what millions of sports fans, players and coaches might believe, you won't find any passage that reads, "Participants are free to gain any additional advantage they can — ethical or otherwise — outside of these rules so long as they don't get caught."

Most of the time gamesmanship *is* cheating. It usually involves finding a loophole in the rules and then driving a Zamboni through it. Once upon a time, a player at the Carlisle Indian School, Jim Thorpe's *alma mater*, sprinted through 11 befuddled defenders with the football stuffed in the back of his jersey. A minor league catcher once picked off a runner with a potato. More recently, retired coaching legend Bo Schembechler had the players on his Michigan football team place washers between their regulation half-inch cleats and the soles of their shoes to give them more traction. Incidents like those might be construed as more cheeky than harmful. They involve using a little creativity to gain an edge. Shortly after something like that happens, a rules committee usually decides how to plug the hole and everyone moves on.

Every time sins like those succeed, they contribute to the attitude that deliberate fouls are worth the risk and the penalty if you still win. That beats the growing consequences of losing. And there are at least some people out there who feel officials are complicitous because they're not taking a firmer stand.

Getting caught cheating really involves two things: actually doing something illegal and then having an official step up and take action. More often than ever, the problem with that sequence is not the breaking of rules but the official taking effective action.

Any official worth his or her salt will penalize a blatant act of cheating, but what about dealing with cheating or unethical behavior that's not so clear-cut? In football, is an offensive lineman who holds his opponent, knowing that such an act is illegal, cheating or is he just gambling he won't get caught? Is there even a difference? What about the basketball player who flops hard to the floor after minimal contact? Is he cheating?

U.S. Team Cheats for Victory

Everyone remembers the indelible images of the U.S.'s dramatic victory in the 1999 Women's World Cup. Few remember how we ultimately obtained that victory.

During the penalty kicks, U.S. goalie Briana Scurry violated the rule that says the goalie is allowed to move only laterally along the goalline prior to the kick being attempted. When Scurry made her game-ending save, she clearly darted forward at the Chinese kicker a good two strides — thereby greatly diminishing the angle the kicker had on the goal — before batting the ball away.

Afterward, when asked about it by a *Los Angeles Times* reporter, Scurry said she had cheated, and added, "It is only cheating when you get caught."

As it turns out, Scurry had premeditated her move by testing the referee, Nicole Mouidi-Penigat of Switzerland, on the first penalty kick, taking a modified run forward before the ball was kicked to see whether or not her action would be called. When it wasn't, she went for the big play two shots later and it paid off in a victory.

L.A. Times editor Bill Dwyre wrote, "Of the mail received at the *Times* in the aftermath of a series of stories on this tainted victory, the most-frequently heard refrain was that it was the responsibility of the referee to call the play and since she didn't, there need be no moral or ethical discussion."

Officials have fallen into the trap of trying to give their sports what they think they want rather than simply enforcing the rules as written. That often stems from their belief that leagues want officials who don't upset the flow of the game by calling fouls that have become common events.

Foul Language

Ron Luciano, the late AL umpire, once wrote that dealing with offensive language from players and managers is one of the toughest judgments in sports. "One man's swear word is another man's adjective," was his position.

Language can be a tough gray area for officials, for anyone for that matter. What's offensive to me may not be offensive to you, for example. Some people may be appalled at any remark that takes the Lord's name in vain; others might find more crude words, such as one in particular beginning with the letter 'f,' as the height of foul language; still others may view slurs that disparage ethnic or racial origins as the really, *really* bad words.

High school rulemakers have long made foul language and other unsportsmanlike acts points of emphasis. It seems every year, from sport to sport, there's additional instruction about sporting behavior. Does all that emphasis on eliminating foul language mean we should expect record numbers of ejections? Not necessarily. Before the penalty comes the act: If you work to discourage foul language, who needs enforcement?

Preventive officiating begins before the game starts. In Iowa, like a growing number of jurisdictions, the referee carries a printed sportsmanship statement on a little blue card. The state expects the official to read it to the head coach and captains during the pregame meeting. Anyone hearing the statement who is smart enough to be a head coach or captain should conclude that unacceptable language isn't going to be tolerated.

Once the game starts, the good official can see trouble brewing. It can be two teammates muttering between themselves. Maybe a head turns toward an opponent as he walks past. A player bleeps to himself a little severely after a dropped pass. A good coach can see it coming, too. If the officials don't take action on the warning signs when they reach that point, everybody suffers. That's because if the expectations are set during the pregame, it now looks like they weren't serious.

If you don't believe cracking down on profanity works, take a look at the Iowa High School Athletic Association (IHSAA). The 2003-04 school year saw the fewest ejections in the state since 1991. In fact, there were 40 percent less in sports in which the data has been kept since then — football, basketball, baseball and wrestling. The IHSAA attributes the change to the preventive stand officials and coaches took against profanity.

A Primer for Cracking Down on Foul Language

When it comes to foul language, what parameters should officials follow? Here are some suggestions:

❏ **Volume:** If the obscenity is shouted loudly enough for spectators or other non-participants to hear, assess the appropriate penalty (technical foul, 15-yard penalty, etc.). You might not wish to convey you are so tolerant you will ignore obvious violations. Conversely, if the profanity is uttered so quietly you are the only one to hear it, a warning may be a sufficient reaction.

❏ **Context:** Sometimes it's not what someone says, but how they say it. Obviously, you should penalize the player who swears as part of a personal verbal assault, e.g. "You are f——— brutal!" If the profanity is phrased differently and in a one-on-one conversation, some leeway is appropriate. Most officials would let a comment such as, "I just think that's a horses— rule," pass with only a suggestion the player use different language to convey his complaint. Likewise, an under-the-breath reaction to a misplay would be best ignored.

❏ **Background:** Keep in mind the phrase, "When in Rome, do as the Romans do." Players from "rougher" areas should not be given carte blanche, but a little latitude is often called for in such situations.

❏ **Level of play:** The younger the player, the shorter the leash. Swearing is habitual. It is naïve to think a peewee league player who is penalized today won't utter an onfield curse at the next level, but it sends a message that officials at all levels of play will have little tolerance for swearing.

2

The Fallout of Poor Sportsmanship on Officials

In this chapter ...

- **A Nationwide Officiating Shortage**
  Why are officials leaving the avocation?

- **Officials' Personal Safety**
  The impact of poor sportsmanship on officials' personal safety.

It's easy for officials to say that poor sportsmanship is not their problem. After all, officials are on the field or court to do a specific job, and that job has little to do with fostering the values of good sportsmanship. That's something for the coaches to worry about.

While most would agree that coaches do indeed have the biggest responsibility for teaching and modeling good sportsmanship for athletes, it's naïve to think that officials don't play a role in fostering good sportsmanship. We discussed in the last chapter how the actions or non-actions of officials can impact the behavior of the participants. Now let's look at how that behavior significantly impacts officials.

A Nationwide Officiating Shortage

There's a national crisis in officiating: There are not enough officials to cover the ever-increasing number of high school games played in this country. Not enough officials means games must either be cancelled or postponed.

NASO devoted its entire national Summit in 2001 to the subject of recruitment and retention in officiating. The news of a national shortage was presented at a session titled "Why Aren't There Enough Refs?" during which NASO unveiled the results of a nationwide survey of state high school association officiating leaders, the men and women largely responsible for registering and accrediting officials in every sport each state governs. They know the numbers better than anyone.

There was a 100 percent response to the survey; all 60 state association offices answered the survey. (There are 51 state associations, including the District of Columbia, as well as some larger states like California that are broken up into several state association sections). The news was grim.

In the first question on the survey, "In general, does your state have an officials' shortage?" an astounding 90 percent responded yes (54 out of the 60; only Connecticut, Idaho, Iowa, Massachusetts, Oklahoma and Wisconsin responded no).

What was more revealing was why the shortage exists. Poor sportsmanship was the number-one reason cited by state administrators for why officials do not re-register. Poor sportsmanship by spectators was cited by 76 percent of the respondents, while poor sportsmanship by participants (players and coaches) had the second-highest response with 68 percent. Career demands and family were next, tied at 65 percent, and difficulty in advancing was cited by 53 percent.

When asked what the *single* biggest reason is for officials not re-registering, sportsmanship again was number one. Sixteen

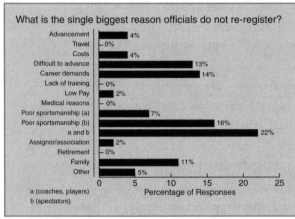

The 2001 NASO Survey

percent said the number-one reason was poor sportsmanship by spectators, 14 percent said it was career demands, 13 percent cited difficulty in advancing, 11 percent attributed it to family demands and another seven percent said it was poor sportsmanship by participants. No other response scored higher than four percent.

At the same time NASO was gathering its information, the NFHS was conducting its own survey. Culling information for the six months leading up to the 2001 NASO Summit, NFHS Assistant Director Mary Struckhoff presented those survey results at the same session.

While the NASO survey endeavored to determine once and for all whether the popular notion that there is a nationwide shortage of officials was correct — as well as try to determine its extent — the NFHS survey struck a more personal chord. It wanted to find out from individual officials why they chose to walk away from a sport they had previously officiated.

After consulting with other officiating leaders, Struckhoff put together a list of 17 potential reasons why officials didn't re-register in a particular sport, plus a write-in "other" section. The results were telling: Most people said it was because of career or job demands, the second most people indicated it had to do with the poor sportsmanship of spectators and third, the poor sportsmanship of participants. Combining the second and third responses, it was clear that poor sportsmanship was the single biggest reason officials did not re-register.

While the two surveys presented at the NASO Summit were specifically aimed at high school officials, it's safe to say that the nationwide shortage doesn't begin and end there. After the success of the state association survey, NASO sent a similar survey to officiating leaders at colleges and universities in charge of intramural and recreational sports.

Out of 55 total respondents, 90 percent answered yes to the question, "In general do intramural and recreational sports have an officials' shortage?" That percentage mirrors the state association response to the same question regarding high school sports. Basketball, flag football and soccer were the intramural or recreational sports most in need of officials.

Fast-forward to 2004, and when a follow-up NASO survey asked officials the question, "Other than physical reasons, what do you believe is the main reason people stop officiating?" 44 percent selected "problems with coaches, players and fans."

It's clear: Poor sportsmanship leads to the attrition of sports officials. But what about the officials who don't leave? Poor sportsmanship impacts them in a big way, too — and in much more

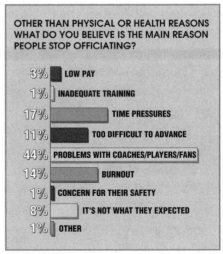

OTHER THAN PHYSICAL OR HEALTH REASONS WHAT DO YOU BELIEVE IS THE MAIN REASON PEOPLE STOP OFFICIATING?

3%	LOW PAY
1%	INADEQUATE TRAINING
17%	TIME PRESSURES
11%	TOO DIFFICULT TO ADVANCE
44%	PROBLEMS WITH COACHES/PLAYERS/FANS
14%	BURNOUT
1%	CONCERN FOR THEIR SAFETY
8%	IT'S NOT WHAT THEY EXPECTED
1%	OTHER

The 2004 NASO Survey

sinister way than simply being an impediment to an otherwise fine competition.

Officials' Personal Safety

We've all had that rough game: Unruly parents on our cases late in the third quarter for a foul call. That annoying father sitting directly behind the plate in the sixth inning, "helping us out" by calling our balls and strikes. Even a parent or coach threatening physical harm after that pass interference call on third and 14 late in the fourth. Sometimes those situations turn ugly. Case in point:

Dontarrius Evans received a sentence of nine months in jail following his felony assault conviction for punching a referee during a recreational basketball game in Long Beach, Calif. The incident happened Sept. 13, 2000, early in the game when the score was only 2-0. Evans, who was upset about a call, struck referee Kevin Robinson when he was looking at the scorers' table. The blow caused permanent damage to Robinson's eye.

At 2-0, one has to ask what happened to cause that fan to

Prevent Future Problems

If you are assaulted or abused, make sure you follow up appropriately with the proper authorities.

☐ **Contact your local police department.** All states have laws against assault and many make special circumstances of assaults on officials. If the police know of the problem, they can respond and prepare better next time.

☐ **Contact your state athletic association.** They have the political clout to effect changes in laws, if necessary. As well, they deal with the schools, which can do a great deal to educate parents, coaches and players.

☐ **Contact your local officials' association.** Those in charge can talk to individual coaches and schools to fix problems at the local level.

For right or wrong, today's environment leaves each of us in a pickle. We love what we do, but no job is worth our health. Stay safe by preventing the problems first. If that isn't possible, try your hand at diplomacy to defuse the situation. If your adversary doesn't take kindly to that approach, it's time to defend yourself, get out of the way and report the problem.

lose it so quickly. Pressure? Was the fan drunk? The answers abound. One thing is apparent: We don't work in our parents' era.

Parents and coaches today have more invested in their children and players than in years past. The scholarship drive now starts earlier than ever, so parents tend to focus their children on fewer sports. There is little room for obstruction. Parents pressure coaches to play their children. Under pressure, coaches are more likely to lash out at an official. Parents are less likely to blame their children than they are the officials for "bad" calls resulting in disqualification, shame or disdain. Uneducated, other parents go along with that blame game, creating a mob mentality — dangerous even for the toughest of officials. Today's environment is such that many officials, veterans and newbies

The 21st Century Pregame

Remember when the pregame meeting consisted of discussing tricky plays, coverage areas, team tendencies and maybe where to go for a postgame meal? You're lucky if you still have the luxury of time to get to those topics. More and more, officials pregame meetings are consumed with issues of safety and security. Here's a checklist of security discussion points for your next pregame meeting:

❑ **An Exit Strategy.** Where will we meet when the game ends? Let's make sure to exit the field or court together. What's the quickest route to the locker room? How can we best avoid spectators when we're leaving?

❑ **The Game Manager.** Who is the game manager? Where is he located? Will he be at the field or court the entire time? We need to prep him on our expectations from him if something gets out of hand.

❑ **The Locker Room.** Is our room private or will coaches be coming and going? Can we arrange for coaches and players to stay out while we're using the room? Are our personal items safe? Will the room be locked after we exit for the game?

❑ **Security Escort.** Will someone be escorting us from the locker room to the field or court? What about to the parking lot after the game?

alike, are quitting officiating for good. And it's discouraging others from starting in the first place.

Where is the civility? It starts and ends with sportsmanship. How people behave — as participants on the field or court or as spectators in the stands or on the sidelines — is an indicator of how safe an official is at any given game.

More and more states nationwide are adopting laws that punish those who subject sports officials to physical or excessive verbal abuse. Illinois became the latest of 17 states to adopt such legislation. Attacking an official can now buy a person up to three years of prison time. The existence of those laws is, among other things, prima facie evidence that assaults on officials are increasing nationally.

While it's good to know that the person who bonked you on the head is in big trouble, it doesn't change the fact that you have a very sore head. In addition to emphasizing that those who assault officials should be punished, the officiating community needs to take steps to ensure that assaults are prevented in the first place. The physical security of officials and their personal property is achieved through a partnership between the officials and the event manager. It is best achieved through a showing of good sportsmanship by all gameday participants.

3

How Officials View the Problem

"I am the referee. It's my job to enforce the rules. Somebody else has to take care of the problem. If the parents would take care of the kids at home, if the coaches would take care of their own players, if the schools and state associations would take care of the coaches, we wouldn't even be talking about poor sportsmanship. Besides, I'm only there for a couple hours a few times a week. What could I possibly do in that little time?"

Sound familiar? A lot of folks complain about the state of sportsmanship these days, but like we saw in the previous chapter, few people have to deal with the fallout of poor sportsmanship more than sports officials. So shouldn't we make it our problem? Shouldn't we concentrate on solutions?

Before we do that, let's take a look at the prevailing attitudes of sports officials regarding sportsmanship. (See the accompaning three charts for a description of the survey respondents.)

NASO Sportsmanship Survey Results

In preparation for the 2004 Summit, NASO surveyed nearly 6,000 sports officials from its membership looking to see how officials viewed the state of sportsmanship. The first 550 responses were used in tabulating the survey results. (Complete

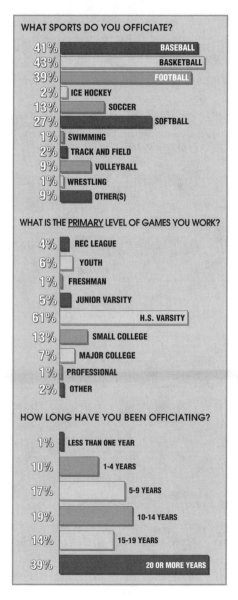

WHAT SPORTS DO YOU OFFICIATE?

41%	BASEBALL
43%	BASKETBALL
39%	FOOTBALL
2%	ICE HOCKEY
13%	SOCCER
27%	SOFTBALL
1%	SWIMMING
2%	TRACK AND FIELD
9%	VOLLEYBALL
1%	WRESTLING
9%	OTHER(S)

WHAT IS THE PRIMARY LEVEL OF GAMES YOU WORK?

4%	REC LEAGUE
6%	YOUTH
1%	FRESHMAN
5%	JUNIOR VARSITY
61%	H.S. VARSITY
13%	SMALL COLLEGE
7%	MAJOR COLLEGE
1%	PROFESSIONAL
2%	OTHER

HOW LONG HAVE YOU BEEN OFFICIATING?

1%	LESS THAN ONE YEAR
10%	1-4 YEARS
17%	5-9 YEARS
19%	10-14 YEARS
14%	15-19 YEARS
39%	20 OR MORE YEARS

survey results can be found on p. 88.) The big question and perhaps most revealing was, "Do you agree with this statement: 'Poor sportsmanship is the number-one problem in our games today?'" The resounding majority (76 percent) of respondents answered in the affirmative.

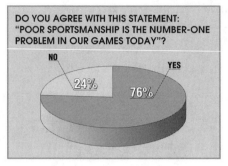

DO YOU AGREE WITH THIS STATEMENT: "POOR SPORTSMANSHIP IS THE NUMBER-ONE PROBLEM IN OUR GAMES TODAY"?

The survey revealed much about the attitudes of officials when it comes to sportsmanship. Most respondents to the survey indicated that poor sportsmanship wasn't getting any better and, in fact, was getting worse (47 percent said the sportsmanship trend over the past five years has gotten slightly worse or gotten a lot worse; 26 percent said it's stayed about the same; and 17 percent indicated it is slightly better).

But the men and women who work in the trenches, it seems, don't feel they can impact the current state of affairs as much as they might like. When asked which group of people has the most responsibility for improving sportsmanship, respondents overwhelmingly pointed to coaches (64 percent). Administrators (15 percent), players (14 percent), fans (five percent) and media (one percent) were also cited. Only two percent of respondents felt officials had the most responsibility.

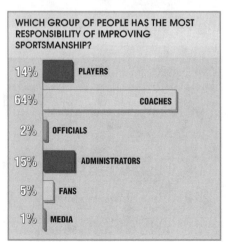

AT THE PRIMARY LEVEL YOU WORK, WHAT HAS BEEN THE SPORTSMANSHIP TREND OVER THE PAST FIVE YEARS? SPORTSMANSHIP HAS:

WHICH GROUP OF PEOPLE HAS THE MOST RESPONSIBILITY OF IMPROVING SPORTSMANSHIP?

A follow-up question asked, "Which group of people is best positioned to have the greatest impact on sportsmanship?" Again, coaches were most often cited (65 percent). But interestingly, officials crept up to five percent. Players (12 percent), administrators (10 percent), media (six percent) and fans (two percent) rounded out the responses.

Obviously officials want to invest in the sportsmanship solution as evidenced by another survey question in which 65 percent of respondents indicated they don't believe that officials and their associations do enough to help improve sportsmanship. A whopping 89 percent of respondents indicated that they consider themselves "partners with players, coaches and administrators in establishing an atmosphere of good sportsmanship in a game" (as opposed to simply being enforcers of the rules). Clearly there is a desire on the part of officials to help make the sportsmanship landscape better. So what's holding officials back?

When asked if officials have the tools, such as training, authority, knowledge and courage, to make a significant impact on improving sportsmanship, more than half the

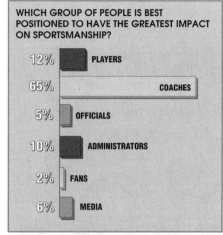

WHICH GROUP OF PEOPLE IS BEST POSITIONED TO HAVE THE GREATEST IMPACT ON SPORTSMANSHIP?

12% PLAYERS
65% COACHES
5% OFFICIALS
10% ADMINISTRATORS
2% FANS
6% MEDIA

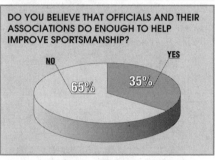

DO YOU BELIEVE THAT OFFICIALS AND THEIR ASSOCIATIONS DO ENOUGH TO HELP IMPROVE SPORTSMANSHIP?

NO YES
65% 35%

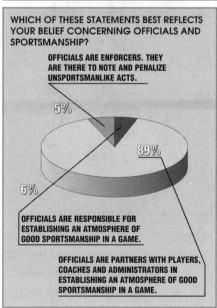

WHICH OF THESE STATEMENTS BEST REFLECTS YOUR BELIEF CONCERNING OFFICIALS AND SPORTSMANSHIP?

OFFICIALS ARE ENFORCERS. THEY ARE THERE TO NOTE AND PENALIZE UNSPORTSMANLIKE ACTS.

5%

89%

6%

OFFICIALS ARE RESPONSIBLE FOR ESTABLISHING AN ATMOSPHERE OF GOOD SPORTSMANSHIP IN A GAME.

OFFICIALS ARE PARTNERS WITH PLAYERS, COACHES AND ADMINISTRATORS IN ESTABLISHING AN ATMOSPHERE OF GOOD SPORTSMANSHIP IN A GAME.

respondents (54 percent) said yes. If that's the case, what, then, is the problem? The answer might be found in a follow-up

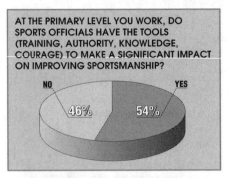

question — "What tool do officials most lack when it comes to making a significant impact on improving sportsmanship?" Nearly half (46 percent) of the respondents — who are all officials themselves — said courage.

The results beg the question: Have we lost that in officiating? Has it gotten to the point where we don't have the courage to take care of business anymore? Again, responses came from working officials, not coaches or administrators.

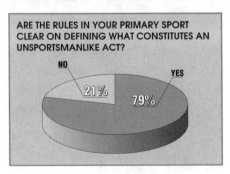

Officials responding to the question, "Do leaders of organized sports at all levels have a common vision for improving sportsmanship in our games?" answered no (76 percent). Relating another survey question that asked if officials were satisfied with the level of support they receive from their assigners or supervisors when penalizing acts of poor sportsmanship, 65 percent of respondents said no. That could be seen as the crux of the issue. Officials know poor sportsmanship is a problem, but nobody wants to

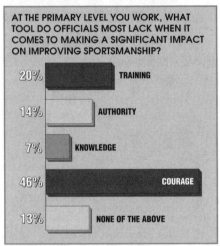

be the lone referee or umpire who steps up and penalizes such behavior. In chapter one, we took a close look at some of those behaviors by game particpants that are getting out of control —

such as cheating, rough play and foul language. Officials can directly impact such behavior by using their power to penalize such acts.

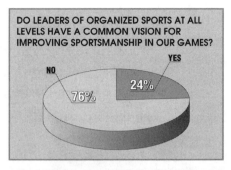

DO LEADERS OF ORGANIZED SPORTS AT ALL LEVELS HAVE A COMMON VISION FOR IMPROVING SPORTSMANSHIP IN OUR GAMES?

NO 76% — YES 24%

But the NASO survey indicates many officials feel they will not be supported if they do. Or they will be out of step if they do. While it's easy to say, "Let's just take care of business and clean up our sports," the reality is officials generally will not jeopardize future assignments by making calls beyond what is universally accepted by particpants and administrators. For example, if high school basketball in a large metropolitan area has accepted a

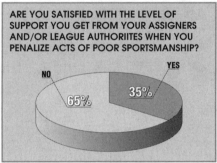

ARE YOU SATISFIED WITH THE LEVEL OF SUPPORT YOU GET FROM YOUR ASSIGNERS AND/OR LEAGUE AUTHORIITES WHEN YOU PENALIZE ACTS OF POOR SPORTSMANSHIP?

NO 65% — YES 35%

certain amount of physical play for years and years, and in fact has a reputation for producing tough, physical players, how will the official who suddenly decides to start penalizing such play be viewed?

Effectively, the survey indicated that officials feel they do have the tools available to impact sportsmanship, but they 1) lack the courage to use those tools, and 2) often don't feel their bosses will support them when they do use those tools.

Those results may not surprise some of you who have been reading the news section of *Referee* magazine or other media publications. "Player Punches Hoops Ref" and "Youth Game Called When Parent Loses Control" are the types of headlines that regularly make news these days. Maybe you've seen the decline of sportsmanship first-hand in your own games — youngsters who regularly complain about calls or players and coaches who do *anything* to win a game.

So who is to blame? More importantly, who is responsible for impacting change? The 2004 survey revealed that officials feel there's plenty of blame to go around.

Whose Job is It?

As we've seen, sports officials want and accept a portion of responsibility for improving sportsmanship. Realistically, our influence extends to the game itself and the participants during the

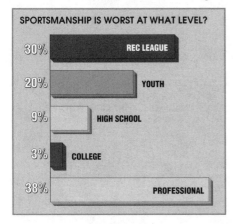

SPORTSMANSHIP IS WORST AT WHAT LEVEL?

30%	REC LEAGUE
20%	YOUTH
9%	HIGH SCHOOL
3%	COLLEGE
38%	PROFESSIONAL

game. When it comes to impacting the internal attitudes of participants, other folks are in much better positions to impact behavior.

Thirty-eight percent of respondents believe that sportsmanship is worst at the pro level. It's one thing if pro athletes are exhibiting poor sportsmanship in their own games, but a majority of the respondents believe that the poor behavior is influencing the lower levels. In fact, 77 percent of respondents said that the acts of poor sportsmanship at the higher levels of sport have a huge effect on sportsmanship at the lower levels. If young people try to emulate their favorite

SPOTLIGHT ON ...
Positive Coaching Alliance
Positive Coaching Alliance (PCA) is a nonprofit organization based at Stanford University with the mission to transform youth sports so sports can transform youth. PCA was created to transform the culture of youth sports to give all young athletes the opportunity for a positive, character-building experience.

It has three national goals:

1. To replace the "win-at-all-cost" model of coaching with the "Double-Goal Coach" who wants to win but has a second, more important, goal of using sports to teach life lessons:

2. To teach youth sports organization leaders how to create an organizational culture in which Honoring the Game is the norm: and professionals' athletic moves, it shouldn't be surprising that they might try to emulate them is other ways as well.

"I think it starts with us," said Mike Pereira, NFL director of officiating, during a sportsmanship session at the 2001 NASO Summit. "Whether it's the NFL, the NBA, Major League Baseball or the National Hockey League, people watch us on Sunday afternoons, kids emulate what athletes do. The pros and college sports have a huge impact on the play of the game at the lower levels. To turn our backs on that is a huge mistake."

Pereira explained that the NFL has gathered data on how the actions of its players have a direct

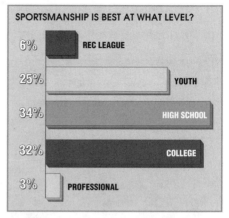

SPORTSMANSHIP IS BEST AT WHAT LEVEL?
6% REC LEAGUE
25% YOUTH
34% HIGH SCHOOL
32% COLLEGE
3% PROFESSIONAL

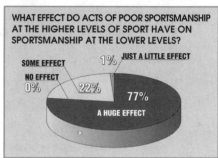

WHAT EFFECT DO ACTS OF POOR SPORTSMANSHIP AT THE HIGHER LEVELS OF SPORT HAVE ON SPORTSMANSHIP AT THE LOWER LEVELS?
JUST A LITTLE EFFECT 1%
SOME EFFECT
NO EFFECT
0% 22%
77% A HUGE EFFECT

3. To spark and fuel a "social epidemic" of Positive Coaching that will sweep this country.

There are many people in this nation who want to change the culture of youth sports, but they do not feel equipped to do so. Positive Coaching Alliance has developed practical tools to change the culture of youth sports and is making them available to coaches, parents, league organizers and others who will fire this movement.

Positive Coaching Alliance provides live, research-based training workshops and practical tools for coaches, parents and leaders who operate youth sports programs to get them on the same page about what it means to honor the game. Positive Coaching Alliance educates adults who shape the youth sports experience by offering partnership programs with YSO's, schools, cities and national sports governing bodies. PCA also provides corporations with the opportunity to offer sports parent workshops to their employees.

bearing on young athletes. "(When) the throat slash gesture had sneaked into our game," he said, "the minute we saw that, we knew we had to address it. (Then-NFL Senior Director of Officials) Jerry Seeman got involved, and got with the officials, and said this is going to be a foul if we ever see it, no matter whether it's directed at another player or just directed at the crowd. There's nothing good that comes from it. No more than three weeks after (the throat slash gesture) appeared, we received a video from a Southern California high school official who sent it in so he could be evaluated by one of our guys. Lo and behold, there was a quarterback sack, and the high school kid who made the sack, got up and (made the throat slashing gesture). No secret where it came from."

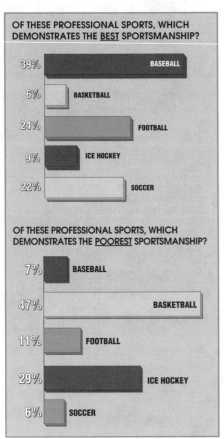

OF THESE PROFESSIONAL SPORTS, WHICH DEMONSTRATES THE BEST SPORTSMANSHIP?

- 39% BASEBALL
- 6% BASKETBALL
- 24% FOOTBALL
- 9% ICE HOCKEY
- 22% SOCCER

OF THESE PROFESSIONAL SPORTS, WHICH DEMONSTRATES THE POOREST SPORTSMANSHIP?

- 7% BASEBALL
- 47% BASKETBALL
- 11% FOOTBALL
- 29% ICE HOCKEY
- 6% SOCCER

NFHS Executive Director Bob Kanaby agreed with Pereira's assessment. "We can give you examples of the first headbutt we saw from a student-athlete," he said. "We saw it at a professional basketball game, and then almost immediately after that we saw it (at the high school level). ... Younger people look at older people, or even older siblings, and emulate what they do."

Professional athletes may influence younger athletes when it comes to sportsmanship, but officials surveyed believe the most responsibility for improving sportsmanship lies with coaches (64 percent), the people who are teaching and interacting with the athletes regularly. They serve as the close-up role models.

Some respondents also felt a lot of responsibility lies with administrators (15 percent) and the players (14 percent) themselves.

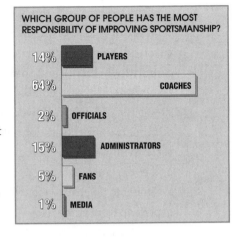

WHICH GROUP OF PEOPLE HAS THE MOST RESPONSIBILITY OF IMPROVING SPORTSMANSHIP?

14% PLAYERS
64% COACHES
2% OFFICIALS
15% ADMINISTRATORS
5% FANS
1% MEDIA

Kanaby and the NFHS have the most direct contact with the student-athletes who hold the promise of that future. And there are more high school athletes than any other group of athletes. The equation is simple: A whole lot of kids play high school sports; a fraction of those kids get to compete at the college level; and a small fraction of those kids eventually go on to professional sports, where the trickle down behavior starts all over again.

The need for high school students to learn sportsmanship is crucial. "We have to constantly reinforce in our own minds the fact that sportsmanship is a learned behavior," said Kanaby. "Whereas we have our classroom activities to teach math skills, English skills, language skills and the like, we use our playing fields and gymnasiums to teach other skills of life — respecting your opponent, respecting yourself and doing all the kinds of things that tend to make you better prepared to face life. Sportsmanship, then, becomes the curriculum of the sports activities in that school. You learn to deal with defeat. You learn to deal with victory. And you learn all those other parameters that basically help you deal with what life is going to give you.

"We fail a youngster if on a Friday night he passes for 300 yards, and then on Saturday night he beats up his girlfriend. We fail that youngster in terms of understanding what they really should gain from participation in sports. We have to decide very clearly whether we want to educate young people to be All-American football, basketball or other sports players, or if we want them to be basically good people who are ready to contribute to our society."

Toward that end, the NFHS identified six groups of people who factor into sporting behavior. "The first group is the coaches," said Kanaby, "because coaches are the first line in terms of whether or not something is going to be acceptable, or something is not acceptable relative to behavior. The second group are officials, followed by school administrators, athletic administrators, the student-athletes themselves, and, most recently identified as being a real source of need on our part and everyone's part, are parents and fans. Those six core groups are going to determine what the outcome of these educational experiences are going to be — positive or negative."

As far as how high school officials can be involved in that process, Kanaby said, "If (officials) embrace and believe in the fact that a playing field or a gymnasium floor is a classroom setting, much like a math class is during the course of the day for that youngster, then an official plays an important part in terms of keeping order, in terms of making certain that the game is played within the rules."

SPOTLIGHT ON ...
Citizen Through Sports Alliance (CTSA)
The Citizenship Through Sports Alliance is the largest coalition of professional and amateur athletics organizations in the United States, focused on character in sport.

CTSA promotes fair play at all levels — youth leagues to professional sport — to reinforce the value of sport as a test of character. Since 1997, CTSA has been building a sports culture that encourages respect for self, respect for others and respect for the game.

Annual Citizenship Through Sports Awards recognize selected athletes' outstanding citizenship, sportsmanship, ethical conduct and community service. Proceeds benefit alliance initiatives and Stay in Bounds character-education programs.

Currently, membership of the Citizenship Through Sports Alliance is comprised of 12 organization, including the major professional

But the educational process by its nature is no overnight solution. It takes time and patience to teach and accept those notions. "If we're making any progress on this at all nationwide," said Kanaby, "it's on the playing field itself, because we have control over players, we have control over coaches, we have input to officials, we have control over administrators to some degree."

The coach is the first line of enforcement of good behavior; but the coach can also be the first line of acceptance of poor behavior. "This whole value analysis we're discussing, nobody can argue with integrity and honesty and all that," said Pereira. "All those values are common sense, and we could all come up with them as goals to achieve, but I look at responsibility. Who is responsible for making a situation a more positive situation for the officials? It's coaches. They have to be responsible. They should be the people who lead by example. If the coach is allowed to berate an official, or if he has an over-emphasis on winning and possibly skirting the rules to win, then we're going to have a hell of a tough time trying to teach kids right from wrong."

leagues — NFL, NBA, NHL and Major League Baseball — the NFHS, the NCAA and the U.S. Olympic Committee among others. Representatives from those organizations participate as members of the Board of Directors. The common bond between all groups is their desire and determination to focus on ethical conduct in athletics, cultivating and maintaining a respectful sports culture, and enhancing the values of citizenship in their own organizations as well as influencing others in communities across the country. CTSA has a Corporate Advisory Board that provides guidance to CTSA and assists with its fund development efforts.

CTSA's website — www.sportsmanship.org — features links to alliance members and "It's Up to Us," a community-organizing tool kit for grass-roots community efforts to teach, learn and practice good citizenship. The tool kit is "user friendly," with a menu of ideas, activities and materials geared to community needs.

Kanaby agreed with Pereira's assessment and added, "The coach is the key. The coach will always be the key. The coach has always been the key. But we've seen a dramatic change in our coaching staffs in this country."

According to Kanaby, it's no longer the norm to have a teacher-coach who is an authority figure involved with and seen by the students all throughout the school day. Instead, coaches are coming from elsewhere in the community and may not even show up on school grounds until after the regular school day is finished.

"It's extremely difficult to provide the (sports as an educational experience) message to those individuals unless school administrators and athletic administrators are designing programs that actually bring those individuals in at some particular time of the year, and say, 'Here is why we have these sports programs in our schools,'" said Kanaby. "'It's not to win the state championship, it's not to win the league championship, it's not to do all those things. They're great byproducts to what happens, but the real reason is education.'

SPOTLIGHT ON ...
Tracking Conduct Fouls

Chuck Mitrano, commissioner of the Division III Empire 8 Conference in Rochester, N.Y., applied for and received a grant for the 2003-04 school year that has all Division III conferences track what he terms "conduct fouls" in 17 different sports (football, baseball, softball, wrestling, field hockey, and men's and women's basketball, volleyball, soccer, water polo, ice hockey and lacrosse).

What are conduct fouls? Mitrano, who was named a sports ethics fellow by the Institute of International Sport, says they are any type of foul that stems from unacceptable behavior as opposed to basic rules infractions.

It seems pretty simple, tracking data. But Mitrano has evidence that his system works. Before going Division-wide with the initiative, Mitrano conducted the same sort of conduct foul tracking within his own conference for two years. In the course of that time, Empire 8

"I've talked to athletic administrators who say 75 percent of their coaches are not in their school building. They come there at three o'clock or later. They don't see any of the students all day. The kids don't see any of them all day. Don't get me wrong, to be very frank, we have a lot of teacher-coaches who are in schools all day, and they do a horrific job. We would be better off without them. But it's generally better (if I'm a coach) if I see my team in the halls, if I see them in the cafeteria and I talk to them. I'm building a bond."

The process of improving sportsmanship isn't going to happen overnight, but it is happening. Individuals and organizations at all levels of competition realize the need for it; they see the poor behavior on the part of the athletes, coaches and spectators; they see the droves of officials leaving the profession. But officials should not simply sit back and passively wait for their lot to improve.

"Everything is connected," said NCAA Senior Vice-President and Chief Operating Officer Boggan, now retired. "If you think

men's and women's soccer teams received 25 percent fewer yellow cards and 20 percent fewer red cards last fall than during the previous season.

It's not easy to quantify sporting behavior, says Mitrano, but tying real data to poor behavior "helps us all understand and model good sportsmanship."

Similarly, the Wisconsin Intercollegiate Athletic Conference (WIAC) received a $39,000 grant from the NCAA in 2001 to conduct a comprehensive study on sportsmanship and character in sports. A primary objective of the study was to define appropriate behaviors in a competitive sports setting, and shared responsibilities for modeling positive character in sport.

The National Association of Division III Athletic Directors posted a detailed report of the WIAC initiative on its website at http://nadiiiaa.uaa.rochester.edu/Resource%20Documents/WIAC_Character_Report.htm.

it's not, you're probably not aware of the way the world works. Everyone has an opportunity to impact this situation, and clearly officials can and should do it in ways that are comfortable for them. It may be only one time, but you see officials talking to players, football, volleyball, baseball, every sport. Those conversations can be educational, or they can just be fluff. Maybe you will only see this kid one time, and you may say, 'Hey, you know if you keep that up, you're not likely to be playing in this league very long.' Everyone has a responsibility for changing the culture."

SPOTLIGHT ON ...

NCAA Committee on Sportsmanship and Ethical Conduct

In 1997, the NCAA's member schools and conferences established a Committee on Sportsmanship and Ethical Conduct, representing educational institutions from all three Divisions. The committee's mission is to improve the condition of sportsmanship and ethical conduct in all aspects of intercollegiate athletics by developing and implementing strategies that foster greater acceptance of the value of respect, fairness, civility, honesty and responsibility.

Nearly 150 representatives from intercollegiate athletics, higher education and other key constituent groups convened in Dallas Feb. 20, 2004 for the Sportsmanship and Fan Behavior Summit. The summit was organized by the Collegiate Commissioners Association, individuals from the membership and NCAA national office staff. The summit's purpose was threefold: (1) to examine issues related to fan

So let's recap: Poor sportsmanship is a problem. The survey results are clear. Who is at fault and who is responsible for improving sportsmanship is clear as well. Everyone plays a part. But since the survey was posed to officials, a questions remains: How can officials help improve sportsmanship? The bottom line is that more can be done by officials to improve sportsmanship. It's time to look in the mirror. What are you doing?

---

violence at or in conjunction with collegiate sporting events; (2) to raise awareness and initiate national communication among key stakeholders; and (3) to identify possible best practices that can be compiled into a report for local application.

It is strongly encouraged that key administrators (e.g., chief executive officer, coaches, game management staff, risk management staff, student-athletes, student leaders, local police and government representatives) should convene to review and discuss issues and policies related to sportsmanship and fan behavior in intercollegiate athletics at your institution.

A report was generated as a result of the summit and a video was created to help illustrate the nature and seriousness of the issues related to sportsmanship and fan behavior that have the potential to impact every institution and its campus community.

You can download the report and video for free at: http://www2.ncaa.org/legislation_and_governance/eligibility_and_conduct/sportsmanship.html

4

The Official's Role in Improving Sportsmanship

In this chapter ...

- **Arguments for Involvement**
  Why we need to be proactive in addressing poor sportsmanship.

- **Using the Tools at Hand**
  Selective rule enforcement and inconsistencies to lead to future problems.

Arguments for Involvement

Based on the survey results we saw last chapter, it's clear that many officials have an interest in becoming involved in solving behavior-related problems. If you're still not convinced that as an official you do have a role in improving officiating, the following arguments will help:

Time to Step Up

By John Kimmel, president of AOA Sports in San Antonio and active NCAA Division I volleyball referee

Every sport has a codified set of rules. Generally, those rules are divided into such areas as administration, protocol, game play and officials' responsibilities. In all cases those directives are based upon fundamental values such as fairness, honesty and integrity. In youth sports, elements of having fun and character development are also essential and critical elements of the rules of the game and its complementary code of conduct.

As officials, we are entrusted with the enforcement of the rules of play and the code of conduct of the game. Over the last several years, we have continually reduced our attention on the character development issues of the game while concentrating on the technical aspects of the rules of play, mechanics and positioning. That has lead to an increase in unmanaged unsportsmanlike behavior by coaches, players and fans. Essentially, we have abrogated our responsibility to enforce the intrinsic values of sportsmanship.

We continue to blame others for the deteriorating climate of sportsmanship while not looking at our role and examining our failure to halt the slide into uncivilized conduct. We expect administrators, coaches, fans, players and parents to show respect for the game and to act in a sporting manner; yet we officials continue to allow unsporting behavior to escalate to a loud crescendo before we step in with any corrective action. Simply put, we don't get involved until it's too late.

What then is sportsmanship? Sportsmanship is a melding of several core values that almost everyone believes should guide the conduct of all involved in the game. Those values include compassion, acceptance, honesty, integrity, pride, humility and understanding. One way players, fans and parents demonstrate sportsmanship when they win is to do so with grace, without over jubilation, and when they lose to do so with dignity without blaming others.

If sportsmanship is accepting the outcome without gloating or blaming, what then is the official's role in developing, maintaining and supporting a climate where sportsmanship prevails? I believe our role is to establish clear, consistent and concise behavioral boundaries based upon the intent and philosophy of the code of conduct of the game in addition to its rules. Bench and onfield or oncourt decorum must have as high a priority as we place on rule application, mechanics, positioning and the other things we use to officiate any sporting contest.

I have yet to find any rule in any sport that states the coach may yell at the referee, continually question judgment calls and otherwise express displeasure with the way the game is called. The same holds true for players. Generally, the rules allow for coaches or team captains to discuss certain aspects of the game in a professional, non-demeaning, non-confrontational manner. As a matter of fact, we generally give more latitude to the coach than to the players. Most sets of rules contain codes of conduct or codes of behavior for coaches and for players. Administrators have specific responsibilities related to establishing and maintaining a safe and positive sporting environment for everyone associated with the game. Over the last few years, many rule governing bodies have made sportsmanship a special emphasis item.

How did we get here? Over the years, officials' camps, clinics and meetings have been preaching an ever-increasing level of tolerance. We are repeatedly told to let coaches and players react to judgment calls and for us not to overreact in those situations. We did that at the request of coaches because for years we did not really let them coach; we made them sit and be quiet. We have simply gone too far the other way now. The result of that constant demand for increased tolerance has lead to an almost complete abrogation of officials managing unsporting behavior. Lately it seems that we don't even get involved until we have a violent act or until the coach has really, *really* lost it.

I agree that we should be approachable, open and understand that emotions run high in our games. I am asking that we begin to step up to our responsibility to enforce the character and value concepts of the sports we chose to officiate. In all sports (youth through college) the rules are part of a highly regarded educational process tied directly to character building and the establishment and reinforcement of a core set of values.

Currently, we are less a part of that developmental process than we should be. Our very presence places us in leadership positions and makes us role models. Our every act, word and deed sends strong messages to all who cheer, coach or play; but it is especially significant to the young impressionable people who play. What message do we send when we let coaches and players continually berate or question our every call? What message do we send when we let folks speak and act with disdain, with disgust or with disrespect?

We cannot do anything about the coach or parent who blames us for his or her loss; but we certainly can do something about establishing a more positive sporting experience. We can also provide the players a positive and decisive role model when it comes to unacceptable behavior. Besides arriving early, having a terrific pregame, being and looking fit, dressing professionally and behaving as this is the most important game we've ever called, we can help build core values by:

1. Dealing with poor bench and onfield or oncourt behavior early in the contest.

2. Making bench and onfield or oncourt behavior a higher priority.

3. Asking our association leaders to work with the administrators and coaches to develop acceptable bench behavior guidelines.** For example, we host an annual meeting with our athletic directors. In that meeting we discuss issues related to leading and managing our respective parts of the sporting events. That has proven to be beneficial to everyone.

4. **Working with administrators when behavior starts to get out of control.** If we believe that a coach is too aggressive or that his or her behavior could cause problems, we call the athletic director and talk about it. We believe that since the athletic director can talk to us about how our officials are doing, we should be able to talk to the athletic director about his or her coaching staff and players.

5. **Understanding ourselves** — our pressure points, our hot buttons, our responses to stressful situations and our non-verbal messages.

6. **Discussing sportsmanship in every camp, clinic and meeting.** We should discuss its importance as a core value and we should discuss what is acceptable and what is not acceptable behavior. We must begin to curb the outrageous behavior of those coaches and players who disrespect the sport, their competition and/or the officials.

7. **Establishing a benchmark on what is or what is not acceptable to you.** For example, I have a 10-year-old grandson and a seven-year-old granddaughter. My personal benchmark centers on whether or not I'd want my grandchildren to act or talk that way to me or to anyone else. After all, I want them to grow up to be adults who have positive values, who act with civility and poise and who manage their anger in a constructive manner. Since they look to me as a role model and since they then act as I act, I know I must act and speak as I wish them to act and speak.

We owe it to ourselves, our coaches and most especially to our players to ensure we are part of a positive sports experience. For the last couple of years, our motto in AOA Sports has been "Let's put sportsmanship back into sports." If each of us practice and enforce positive sporting behavior, we can all achieve that goal. Thereby making each and every sporting contest a positive and enjoyable experience for everyone.

What are you going to do to about your responsibilities concerning sportsmanship? What is your game plan for putting sportsmanship back into sports? Let's turn the tide of uncivil behavior by taking an aggressive step forward in managing all aspects of our games.

The Way It Is ... and Ought to Be

By Ronnie Carter, executive director of the Tennessee Secondary School Athletic Association

There was a quotation from Holman W. Jenkins Jr. in *The Wall Street Journal* in regard to the law and lawyers that went like this: "The law is a crude machine at best and only spits out something approaching justice if its attendants are committed to justice. As lawyering has become less about doing right and more about doing what you can get away with, our standards of acceptable shenanigans — as usual — seem to be in a free fall." As all of us read that quotation, we probably shake our heads and say, "Boy. That's right." But the hard reminder to us is that we are seeing the same things happening in regard to the approach of coaches, athletes and fans to the playing rules in sports and many times to the "rules" of athletics, whether they are playing rules, eligibility rules or just the rules that have been set down by the association through their representatives.

If Jenkins would permit, I would like to think about a new quotation with a few changes in words that are applicable to our situation: "Rules are a crude machine at best and only spit out something approaching justice if its attendants (administrators, coaches, players, etc.) are committed to justice. As rules have become less about doing right and more about doing what you can get away with, our standards of acceptable shenanigans — as usual — seem to be in a free fall." That hits a little harder, but should also make all of us wonder if that is really not what we are seeing more and more.

Many times we justify what we want to do that is against the rules or against what should be our commitment to doing what is right with a lot of lines and clichés that sound pretty good. The best one that is used many times during the course of a year usually runs something like this: "It is in the best interest of the kids," or, "I'm just doing it for the kids." In frustration, many times we use that line of thinking in a direction that would indicate that the people on the other side of the argument who are enforcing the rules must not really care about kids.

Many times I find that is the line that is used to follow what has been either a violation of the rules or some hope that the rules will somehow be set aside. The reality is that that approach or statement becomes a very dangerous approach. If I really think that what I am doing is, in my mind, best for the kids in my program, then I can justify just about anything there is to justify. There really becomes no problem in teaching kids to lie to officials because it accomplishes the goal of winning; there is no problem in helping parents to understand how to get around a particular rule of the athletic association because it is obviously in the best interest of this particular student; on and on it goes.

Holman Jenkins has it all figured out. The commitment to justice is a much greater attribute than any of the rules trying to mandate justice. We refer to that many times with clichés such as, "You can't legislate ethics," but the real lesson for all of us in this activity we call secondary school athletics is to make certain that we are walking our talk and that we are committed to justice and rules with our words and actions as eyes watch all of us daily. To some of us, it seems a tough challenge and a hard journey, but when you examine it, it is really pretty easy and very simple.

Using the Tools at Hand

The words "character" and "sports" used to appear in the same sentence almost as often as "money" and "sports" do now. Whether sports developed character or merely revealed an athlete's character was debatable, but one thing not debatable was that officials needed a strong set of ethics to compensate for players and coaches who may not have had any.

That hasn't changed, not with the increasing rewards that come with victory or gaudy individual statistics; officials must still stand as ramparts of ethical decision-making in stadiums or arenas where some of the very characteristics that sports once nurtured (teamwork, respect for opponents, coaches and officials, composure in the face of adversity, etc.) have now nearly disappeared under assault from a relentless pressure to obtain victory or at least individual recognition at virtually any cost.

Today, sports are laced with intrigue, agendas (hidden and otherwise), rule-stretching, old-fashioned cheating, and other things, such as trash talking and deceptive play. It sometimes seems like enough to make people concerned with ethics throw up their hands and surrender. Josephson's expertise is ethics rather than sports, but he has crafted a second career out of injecting the discussion of ethics into areas often hostile to them, such as business and politics. His career in the law has given him extensive experience in an environment where ethics are often viewed as expendable nuisances rather than inviolate principles.

Several years ago, during the 2000 NASO Summit, a contentious case study emerged concerning balls, strikes and game management, and a spirited discussion between ethicist Michael Josephson and Dave Yeast, NCAA national coordinator of baseball umpires, caught everyone's attention.

Yeast's argument concerned game management. If an umpire is getting a bit too much grief from a pitcher or catcher about strike zone dimensions, he asserted, he or she may watch a pitch slice off the outside corner of the plate and still call "ball" simply to send the message that pitchers pitch, catchers catch and umpires decide. Experienced officials in all sports are likely to perceive that as legitimate game management. Josephson's alternative perspective triggered an interesting exchange.

"In every sport there are things that officials do to maintain control of a baseball game or basketball or football game," said Yeast. "In baseball we are charged with maintaining control of the contest."

"So you can call a ball a strike in order to achieve your goal?" asked Josephson.

"At times, yes," Yeast replied. "I am doing my job as I see fit."

The former attorney and law professor had his follow-up questions ready. "So you're saying that you have the right to lie in order to accomplish a higher purpose?" he asked. "Can you also kick (a player) if that works?"

The audience chuckled, but Yeast answered that by saying using one call out of more than 400 to send a message is legitimate game management while kicking a player is obviously unacceptable. Josephson then took a quick poll of the audience and discovered that many attendees sided with Yeast.

"What else can you do?" continued Josephson. "Can you also call a safe player out? You don't believe in the principle of calling it the way it is or calling it the way you see it. You believe in the principle of calling it the way you want to."

"Absolutely not," answered Yeast. "I am officiating the entire contest. If I'm working the plate in a Division I baseball game, I've got 350 to 400 calls to make."

Neither side ever came to complete agreement, but the question was raised on everyone's mind: How far can you go with game management before you have a material effect on the outcome?

Ethical Officiating: The Rules Rule — The very existence of officiating postulates two things that are contrary to a purely ethical competitive environment: first, in the absence of an authority figure, athletes and coaches will break rules to gain an advantage; second, athletic competition includes vague and ambiguous situations that must be arbitrated by an impartial observer (the "gray area" situations that are resolved by the officials) because players will not self-report infractions and opponents will not agree on a call that puts one of them at a disadvantage. Of course, if people always did the right thing, nobody would need officials.

Since the rules define the boundaries of acceptable (and presumably ethical) behavior as well as the nature of the competition, Josephson believes officials must do more than know and enforce a game's rules: They must revere them.

"Officials are responsible for the integrity of the game," declared Josephson. "The integrity of the game is defined fundamentally by the rules. The rules, as written, must be enforced without regard to whether or not it will please or displease the fans or any particular person. To do otherwise is to be intimidated from doing your job." That statement seems simple and logical enough, but officials know it's not always that easy.

Constitutional scholars would describe Josephson's approach as constructionalist — a literal and essentially non-negotiable reading of the black ink on the white paper of the rulebook. The strike zone extends from here to there, for example, or a hockey player cannot use his stick to impede the progress of another player — no questions asked. The reflexive response from officials to Josephson's ideal: Anyone who has been an official for more than 24 hours knows that rote enforcement of written rules is only part of the job. Any official who relies solely on that skill courts complete disaster.

A literal reverence for the rules seems to be in conflict with the concept of game management, an indispensable skill for officials who wish to succeed at their current level or advance to the next one.

The art and science of game management means applying rules and making decisions that advance competition that is safe and fair for all participants. Basketball is supposedly a non-contact sport, but officials routinely ignore that designation. Rather than wearing out their whistles trying to eliminate contact, officials use their authority to regulate it. Josephson's goal is not to eliminate judgment, but to increase awareness of the sanctity of the rules that do exist. That, he believes, leads to more consistent decisions from one official to another.

Games People Play — We can come to a consensus on some points. For example, when you make a call primarily to placate a bile-spewing coach you're dealing with a question of willpower rather than discernment. Perhaps officials, as a group, can nudge the rulemakers toward a more comprehensive and realistic set of rules.

But even given exceptional rapport between coaches and officials, there will be plenty of gray areas for players and coaches to probe. If ethical behavior is of paramount concern, how do you deal with the trickery and deception that are part and parcel of your chosen sports? Should the rules require that the catcher tell the batter what pitch is coming? Is a successful head fake an ethical violation?

Much of the gray area mischief in sports falls under the heading of "gamesmanship," the art of taking every physical and psychological advantage available in the pursuit of victory. By labeling it "gamesmanship," says Josephson, the sports hierarchy has given it a veneer of legitimacy by implying that such efforts are, in fact, part of the game. Josephson acknowledges that gamesmanship is interwoven with the rules and traditions of various sports, but urges officials to analyze situations through the filter of ethical behavior. The television-inspired growth of trash talking and taunting provides a useful case study.

Gamesmanship is one thing, but what about cheating? How does Josephson apply his ethical framework to athletes who intentionally violate rules to gain an advantage with the hope that they will not be penalized? Officials expect athletes to bend and break rules.

"Policemen expect some people to be burglars and thieves, but that doesn't make it right," he answers. "To expect something means you can predict or anticipate it as being something that people do. The question of ethics is what one *should* do. It would be naïve for a referee not to expect that no matter what the rules are, a certain percentage of people playing a game will try to get an advantage."

Josephson is aware that officials alone cannot change the ethical culture of sports.

The sport does not respect the role of officiating. And that means you have to function in that context, knowing that you're underpaid, under-appreciated, and if you do things right, they might dump you.

"But," Josephson concluded, "why do you want to be in this if you're not willing to do it right?"

5

How Officials Can Improve Sportsmanship

In this chapter ...

- **Pursuing Victory With Honor**
  A nationwide plan to improve sportsmanship.

- **The Arizona Experience**
  A state where it all works together.

At first glance it would seem that sports officials already have the power to promote sportsmanship. After all, their uniforms and whistles give them an automatic status of control. But the fact is many officials are so intent on doing their job as game administrators that they are unaware of the possibilities for positive influencing. The element of authority can be used effectively to promote goodwill among game participants.

When a game is in progress, officials can contribute to the spirit of personal consideration with small gestures and pointed statements. The very nature of their roles includes dealing directly with participants.

Officials should recognize good sportsmanship as ardently as they penalize bad sportsmanship. If a batter whose foul ball caused the catcher to discard his mask during a chase to the backstop picks up the mask and hands it back to the catcher, a simple "Thank you" from the umpire recognizes the act and promotes future acts of good conduct. When a football player flies over the pile to avoid hitting a downed runner, a wrestler helps up an opponent when the combatants have gone off the mat and a basketball or soccer player acknowledges hard but accidental conduct with an apology, an official should let the athlete know what a classy gesture it was.

Officials have other means of curtailing ill will between participants. When players bristle after hard but legal contact, positive reinforcement can prevent illegal retaliation. "Hold it. Let's stay calm. No need to be upset," is a preferred technique. "Knock it off! Cut it out!" are surely "cease and desist" messages too, but they don't have to be delivered in an angry manner. Animosity begets animosity, and an official shouldn't contribute to it. The official's role should be that of a gentle persuader, not a harsh disciplinarian.

Officials also have to keep their ears open because today's climate for sports competition is in some ways unhealthy. That is, baiting, taunting and verbal putdowns are considered by some elements of society to be fashionable, even essential. Officials have an obligation to counter such behavior. Sports officials must curb negative gestures, posing and insulting talk. Unfortunately, some officials ignore belligerent and inflammatory remarks from opponents and coaches. Officials have it in their job description to pay attention and to take a stand.

Officials should be aggressive in setting up opportunities to talk to players. Preseason is a good time. Ask a coach if you can address the team, then develop a message that says, "We're in this thing together, and we can work like partners in making each game go smoothly." Such a talk can show players how to address officials during a game, question judgment calls in a non-antagonistic way or ask for clarification of rules and policies. The whole nature of such a discussion is to allay the feelings of participants that officials are their enemies, that a spirit of cooperation can be achieved if each party sets out to be cooperative and congenial.

That concept is inherent in the Josephson Institute's "Pursuing Victory with Honor" campaign, which advocates the "T.E.A.M." approach to fostering proper behavior.

Pursuing Victory With Honor

Sports best achieves its positive impact on participants and society when everyone plays to win. In fact, without the passionate pursuit of victory much of the enjoyment, as well as the educational and spiritual value, of sports will be lost. Winning is important and trying to win is essential. The Pursuing Victory With Honor campaign, though, advocates keeping winning in perspective:

Winning is Important, but Honor is More Important — Quality sports programs should not trivialize or demonize either the desire to win or the importance of actually winning. It is disrespectful to athletes and coaches who devote huge portions of their lives to being the best they can in the pursuit of individual victories, records, championships and medals, to dismiss the importance of victory by saying, "It's only a game." The greatest value of sports is its ability to enhance the character and uplift the ethics of participants and spectators.

Ethics is Essential to True Winning — The best strategy to improve sports is not to de-emphasize winning but to more vigorously emphasize that adherence to ethical standards and sportsmanship in the honorable pursuit of victory is essential to winning in its true sense. It is one thing to be declared the winner, it is quite another to really win.

There is No True Victory Without Honor — Cheating and bad sportsmanship are simply not options because they rob victories of meaning and value and replace the inspirational high ideals of true sport with the degrading and petty values of a dog-eat-dog marketplace. Victories attained in dishonorable ways are hollow and degrade the concept of sport.

Ethics and Sportsmanship Are Ground Rules — Programs that adopt Pursuing Victory With Honor are expected to take whatever steps are necessary to assure that coaches and athletes are committed to principles of ethics and sportsmanship as *ground rules* governing the pursuit of victory. Their responsibilities to demonstrate and develop good character must never be subordinated to the desire to win. It is never proper to act unethically to win.

Benefits of Sports Come From the Competition, Not the Outcome — Quality amateur sports programs are based on the belief that the vital lessons and great value of sports are learned from the honorable pursuit of victory, from the competition itself rather than the outcome. They do not permit coaches or others to send the message that the most important benefits derived from athletic competition can only be achieved when an athlete or a team wins.

The four-point strategy for achieving the objectives of the Pursuing Victory With Honor campaign is captured in the acronym T.E.A.M. — *teach, enforce, advocate* and *model*. Those four elements should guide the design of all elements of programs to promote sportsmanship and foster good character as well as guide interactions with athletes, parents, coaches, officials and spectators.

T **Teach** — Tell children that their character counts — that their success and happiness will depend on who they are inside, not what they have or how they look. Tell them that people of character know the difference between right and wrong because they guide their thoughts and actions by six basic rules of living (See chapter one for the "Six Pillars of Character" — *trustworthiness*, *respect*, *responsibility*, *fairness*, *caring* and good *citizenship*.) Explain the meaning of those words. Use examples from your own life, history and the news.

E **Enforce** — Instill the Six Pillars of Character by rewarding good behavior (usually, praise is enough) and by discouraging all instances of bad behavior by imposing (or, in some cases, allowing others to impose) fair, consistent consequences that prove you are serious about character. Demonstrate courage and firmness of will by enforcing the core values when it is difficult or costly to do so.

A **Advocate** — Continuously encourage children to live up to the Six Pillars of Character in all their thoughts and actions. Be an advocate for character. Don't be neutral about the importance of character or casual about improper conduct. Be clear and uncompromising that you want and expect your children to be trustworthy, respectful, responsible, fair, caring and good citizens.

M **Model** — Be careful and self-conscious about setting a good example in everything you say and do. Hold yourself to the highest standards of character by honoring the Six Pillars of Character at all times. You may be a good model now, but remember, you don't have to be sick to get better. Everything you do, and don't do, sends a message about your values. Be sure your messages reinforce your lessons about doing the right thing even when it is hard to do so. When you slip (and most of us do), act the way you want your children to behave when they act improperly — be accountable, apologize sincerely and resolve to do better.

Those principles and the "T.E.A.M." concept sound like great ideas, but how do they apply to officials? Based on the Pursuing Victory With Honor principles, Character Counts! Sports put together a variety of athletic codes of conduct to benefit each population segment of the athletic experience. On the Character Counts! website (http://www.charactercounts.org/sports/codes/codes.htm) you can download codes of conduct for athletes, coaches, spectators, parents and officials.

The code for officials of interscholastic-age athletes is as follows:

CODE OF CONDUCT FOR OFFICIALS
TRUSTWORTHINESS

Trustworthiness — Always act so as to encourage and justify trust. Look for opportunities to reinforce the meaning and importance of trustworthiness in players, coaches and parents/guardians.

Integrity — Teach and model the importance of integrity by doing the right thing and making the right call even when the cost is high. Admit mistakes openly and honestly. Enforce the rules as written, as faithfully as they can in a manner consistent with guidelines and interpretations of the rules committee.

Honesty — Be honest and demand honesty. Do not engage in or permit dishonesty by lying, deception or omission.

Reliability — Fulfill commitments. Impress on players and coaches the values of promise keeping and reliability. Demonstrate consistency in the way you enforce the rules throughout the season and during playoffs and championship games, regardless of the potential outcome of the game.

RESPECT

Respect — Treat players, coaches and parents/guardians with respect and require the same of student-athletes and coaches.

Courtesy — Encourage and, where appropriate, require athletes and coaches to treat opponents, teammates and others with respect and courtesy.

Disrespectful Conduct — Seek to control the conduct of parents/guardians, spectators, coaches and players to prevent negative cheers, name-calling, insults, drinking or any other conduct inconsistent with a positive atmosphere of character development. Use proper authority to assure that rules against profanity, trash-talking, taunting, arguing calls and other forms of bad sportsmanship are consistently and strictly enforced. Where appropriate, direct those responsible for game management to exercise control over spectators, bands and spirit groups.

Respect for Coaches — Listen to coaches and others who respectfully and in the appropriate setting wish to discuss the rules, interpretation of the rules or your control over the moral environment of the game.

Sports Experience — Ensure that the sports experience is one of fun and enjoyment. Correct and instruct players in constructive ways. Be generous with praise when it is deserved.

Prejudice — Treat all players as individuals, appreciating their diversity in skills, gender, ethnicity and race. Never permit statements or acts of prejudice.

RESPONSIBILITY

Self-Control — Exercise and demand self-control. Do not fight, scream or otherwise demonstrate uncontrolled anger or frustration. Do not permit players, coaches or spectators to display inappropriate anger.

Grace — Encourage players and coaches to win and lose with grace and dignity.

Accountability — Accept responsibility for your choices of both action and inaction. Those in charge of assigning officials are responsible to: 1) assure that those selected to officiate games are qualified, 2) assure that officials receive training and have been subjected to reasonable character screening, and 3) adopt and enforce rules limiting the number of games an official can work in a specified time.

FAIRNESS

Fair Play — Model and insist on fair play. Make sure all teams compete honorably.

Fair-mindedness — Be open to the ideas, suggestions and opinions of others.

Impartiality — Make all decisions fairly and treat all participants with impartiality. Fair, consistent and competent officiating is essential to a quality basketball program that promotes sportsmanship and fosters respect for the game and the development of good character.

CARING

Concern for Others — Demonstrate concern for others. Discourage selfishness.

CITIZENSHIP

Play By the Rules — Strictly and consistently enforce all rules of the game. Enforce game rules in a manner that advances the goals of sportsmanship, ethics and character building.

The Arizona Experience

Gary Whelchel, former NASO chair and commissioner of officials for the Arizona Interscholastic Association (AIA), takes a hard line with officials who want to scrape responsibility for poor sportsmanship onto someone else's plate.

"Collectively, it is our fault," he said, referring to game officials. "We have allowed things to happen at high school athletic contests that has created turmoil and unsportsmanlike behavior, and we as officials did not use the tools to correct it. Every sport has a tool that allows you to correct poor behavior. Whether it be the flag in football, the technical foul in basketball, the red and yellow cards in soccer and volleyball, you have something that can change the behavior of students and athletes out there on the floor or on the field.

"In our role as officials, we must be part of the solution. We cannot continue to gripe and complain about how bad sportsmanship is today in this country at the high school level, or any level, and not be a part of the solution to correct that problem. We have to do something."

During his Summit session, "Finding Take Charge Solutions," Whelchel revealed how his state, Arizona, has successfully battled poor sportsmanship at the prep level through the Pursuing Victory With Honor program that the AIA instituted three years ago.

"Our basic premise is our officials and our schools work together in a partnership," Whelchel explained. "Our officials stand alongside our 242 high schools in Arizona as partners with them. We are trying to set up and establish an ethical sports culture in Arizona where the whole culture changes. I like to use the analogy with our officials that it's like changing landscapes. You can change flowers, you can trim a tree, but if you really want to change the landscape, you take that big tree and pull the roots out of the ground."

In working together, all AIA officials as well as representatives from all AIA member schools attend a Pursuing Victory With Honor seminar as part of their training. "The schools and the officials are on the same page, working in concert to provide a positive athletic experience that promotes sportsmanship and character building," said Whelchel.

"Walk Worthy in the Uniform" — While AIA schools learn about developing character and values through their coaches and within their student athletes, AIA officials additionally embrace the theme Whelchel has coined for raising expectations and sportsmanship, "Walk Worthy in the Uniform," which is an officiating creed that encompasses professionalism, integrity, ethics and pride.

"We train our officials on what is expected of them," Whelchel said. "And that goes well beyond blowing a whistle and calling fouls. Their job is to set boundaries at the start of the athletic contest that hold the participants accountable for their behavior. (In the state office) we expect officials to handle problems using the tools that are in the book. That's expected of you, to use the tools in the book. If that coach gets out of line or that player gets out of line, they're gone and they sit out the next game. We send a message through our officials that we will not tolerate abuse from the participants in the game.

The Results —

According to Whelchel, the Pursuing Victory With Honor program has been a resounding success in his state. NASO's survey indicated that the biggest cause, other than health or professional reasons, of officials leaving the profession is "Problems with coaches, players and fans" (44 percent). But Whelchel said, "We don't have a problem recruiting officials, and we don't have that problem because we've addressed the one problem that causes officials to leave — poor sportsmanship. We've addressed it. The people who come to officiate for us know that, so we've raised the level of expectations."

AIA Officials Theme and Mission

Our Theme

Officials Are to Walk Worthy in the Uniform:

☐ By following the Code of Ethics, being professional, having the utmost integrity, and possessing an individual quest for excellence in preparation and performance.

☐ By being a positive part of the umpiring community, sharing and growing together for the betterment of umpiring and the game.

☐ By being a part of the educational process, assisting in the education of student-athletes through positive enforcement of sportsmanship guidelines, enforcing rules in a consistent manner, and working with our member schools to enhance the athletic experience.

Our Mission

☐ To provide to our member schools the highest quality umpiring possible with individuals that are properly prepared and trained

☐ To assist in fulfilling our mission to provide quality officiating, and to enhance the evaluation process, officials are to provide to athletic directors and/or coaches a "Promise to Schools" card, which contains our sportsmanship message, reflects our mission, gives names of officials working the contest and requests evaluation from the schools to the AIA regarding the quality of officiating (see p. 70 to view card).

AIA OFFICIALS "PROMISE TO SCHOOLS"

I have...
- Devoted many hours of time, thought and study to the rules of the game
- Accepted all requirements of policy of the AIA
- Prepared myself physically to officiate this athletic contest
- Arrived on time for this contest as per AIA requirements
- Been diligent to wear a proper, clean, and neat uniform

I will...
- Use my position as an official only for the benefit of the student-athlete
- Uphold the honor, dignity, and integrity required of me as a sports official
- Accept my role in this contest in an unassuming manner
- Maintain poise and confidence in managing this contest
- Publicly acknowledge members of the teams and their coaching staff
- Exhibit little or no emotions when dealing with game situations
- Use respectful language when communicating to participants and spectators
- Respond to parents or spectators only when appropriate prior to or after a contest

**I accept and will abide by the Sportsmanship Theme of the AIA,
and will share this message with all participants prior to the contest:**

As officials, we believe that the highest potential in sports is achieved when ALL participants are committed to Pursuing Victory With Honor, and everyone embodies the six core pillars of Respect, Trustworthiness, Responsibility, Caring, Fairness, and Citizenship. To encourage a positive playing environment, we stand alongside our member schools and the coaches, as partners on the same side, supporting sportsmanship, and are in concert with them to provide a positive athletic experience. Please share with your coaches and fellow players that this game will be played under these guidelines.

OFFICIAL	OVERALL RATING 1 - High 5 - Low	RECOMMEND FOR PLAYOFFS
	1 2 3 4 5	Yes No
	1 2 3 4 5	Yes No
	1 2 3 4 5	Yes No
	1 2 3 4 5	Yes No
	1 2 3 4 5	Yes No

SPORT_____DATE_____

SCHOOL_____

COACH/AD_____

Please return to the AIA, 7007 North 18th Street, Phoenix, Arizona, 85020

Registered officials in Arizona increased by nearly 30 percent between 2001-02 and 2003-04, and Whelchel said coach and player ejections are way down, decreasing by 42 percent from 2001-02 to 2003-04 even though the total number of games played significantly increased during that time period.

Registered AIA Officials — Statewide By Sport

	1991-92	1995-96	2001-02	2002-03	2003-04
FOOTBALL	584	612	523	673 (+28%)	681 (+1%)
VOLLEYBALL	289	316	272	368 (+35%)	372 (+1%)
BASKETBALL	782	826	787	984 (+25%)	1,021 (+4%)
SOFTBALL	356	468	375	497 (+32%)	480 (-3%)
BASEBALL	504	559	426	547 (+28%)	547 (0%)
SOCCER	162	220	231	345 (+49%)	339 (-1%)
WRESTLING	137	145	113	123 (+9%)	121 (-2%)
TOTALS	2,814	3,146	2,727 (-15%)	3,537 (+29.7%)	3,561 (+1%)

Arizona, it seems, is a pretty nice place to be an official, but what about that lack of administrative support respondents to the NASO survey indicated in chapter three?

"What you permit, you promote," Whelchel said, referring to his view of officials who don't take care of a sportsmanship-related problem. "If a player comes up and drops the f-bomb on you in the first quarter and you don't do anything, and he drops the bomb in the fourth quarter, and suddenly you do something, what have you taught the child, what have you taught the athlete? You changed character. You take care of that individual in the first quarter, you're not going to have the f-bomb in the fourth, and if you do (take care of it), you don't have that player out there on the field. That's what we tell our officials. More importantly, we support our officials 100 percent in those types of situations. Anything dealing with sportsmanship, our officials are empowered to take care of business. They know that is our expectation (in the state office). They know coaches cannot blackball them.

"I have not had an official in three years tell me that sportsmanship is bad, and what are you, the AIA, going to do about it? — because that is what we heard before: Can't you guys at the AIA take care of poor sportsmanship? Well, you know what? We answered. If you're asking us to take care of it, you'd better buy into the notion that you're part of the problem and you're going to be part of the solution to correct that problem. Our officials understand that is what their job is."

AIA Statistics — Comparing '03 With '04

	2002-03	2003-04	THE DIFFERENCE
NUMBER OF GAMES	36,500	37,600	1,100 MORE GAMES
NUMBER OF EJECTIONS	734	576	158 FEWER EJECTIONS
NUMBER OF EJECTIONS/PER NUMBER OF GAMES	1 EJECTION PER 49 GAMES	1 EJECTION PER 65 GAMES	31% IMPROVEMENT
PERCENTAGE OF GAMES WITH AN EJECTION	2%	1.5%	.5% IMPROVEMENT

Not every location is like Arizona, which has a luxury of control over its officials most places do not since the state office handles all the officiating assignments — throughout both the regular season and postseason — for varsity contests in all sports. Most states have any number of local assigners, league commissioners and supervisors to whom officials must answer. That's in addition to the state office, which licenses officials and holds the keys to postseason assignments.

"Some of you deal with a situation where the roots are so deep and so buried that you can't get to them," said Whelchel recalling his analogy of changing the landscape. "You might find you run into roadblocks and barriers (when you attempt to change the sportsmanship culture in your area), because your system does not allow for that type of change. It takes somebody with power and great leadership to make things work."

It's hopeful to note that the Pursuing Victory With Honor program is by no means confined to Arizona. Hundreds of individual schools, school districts, athletic conferences, and even local officials associations, have adopted the tenets of that program. Other places are adopting a harder line when it comes to poor sportsmanship. In states like Oregon and Florida, schools and sometimes even players are fined significant dollar amounts for such things as ejections or using profanity.

Individual officials, too, can make a difference in the sportsmanship trend, and not just by using the tools at their disposal. As part of Whelchel's "Finding Take-Charge Solutions" session, Summit attendees brainstormed other ways officials can help improve sportsmanship. Suggestions included: setting up programs in local associations to recognize individual youngsters or schools for excellence in sportsmanship, sending in reports to the state office after a problem with a particular school, or conversely, taking the time to write a report for the state office regarding a player or school that showed exemplary sportsmanship, maintaining the highest level of professionalism as officials and getting players directly involved in the behavior of everyone else in the game by stressing to captains their role as leaders of sportsmanship.

Little things individual officials do won't change the entire culture of sports, but in our role as caretakers of the game, officials can help foster an environment that makes it easier for leaders to step up, like they did in Arizona, and make the games "about sportsmanship," as Whelchel said, "not about championships."

Hot Topics
for Officials

In this chapter ...

- **Refs Rating Refs**
  Who is best suited to rate officials?

- **The Impact of Media on Officiating**
  Officiating errors and the public's need to know.

- **Background Checks**
  Are they here to stay?

In addition to discussing the sportsmanship problem throughout most of the 2004 NASO Summit, time was devoted to a variety of hot topics in the officiating community. The issues of evaluations, dealing with the media and background checks each were covered in depth.

Refs Rating Refs

Everybody knows you just can't trust coaches to rate officials. There's too much bias and emotion involved. It's like asking your only heir to pack your parachute, isn't it? Wouldn't we officials do a much better job rating ourselves since we're more objective and know the rules and mechanics?

No.

At least that seems to be the answer in Illinois, where high school coaches and officials both rate officials for playoff assignments. The Illinois High School Association (IHSA) keeps statistics on those ratings, which tell a story that might surprise you: That guy tying your ripcord to an anvil just might be wearing a striped shirt. But he means well.

Here's the scoop: Both officials and coaches had an opportunity to go on the IHSA website and rate officials during the regular seasons for three years (2000-01 to 2002-03). They could rate officials with numbers between one and five, with those numbers correlating to a simple statement:

❑ 1 — This official is qualified to work state final contests.
❑ 2 — This official is qualified to work sectional assignments.
❑ 3 — This official is qualified to work regional assignments.
❑ 4 — This official is qualified to work varsity contests.
❑ 5 — This official is qualified to work underclass contests only.

Those ratings were two of several factors that went into deciding who gets to officiate in the postseason. What surprised people in the IHSA office is that it was the coaches — not the officials — who, as a group, handed in ratings that fit the expectations of a classic bell curve. The officials? Well, they had a tendency to rate their fellows a little high. Perhaps the best example to illustrate that point is this: When rating fellow officials with between one and five years of experience, officials said 48.3 percent of them were qualified to work the state final. With that same group, officials said less than one percent was qualified to work underclass contests only.

Coaches didn't fare a whole lot better, but they were more on target with their ratings: Coaches rating officials with between one and five years experience said 12.3 percent of them were qualified to work state final contests, and 3.1 percent were qualified to work underclass contests only.

The numbers are plain to see. So the conclusion is pretty simple, right? Coaches may not be great at rating officials but at least they're more honest than the officials themselves. Hold on — wasn't it Mark Twain who was fond of saying, "There are three kinds of lies: lies, damn lies and statistics"?

Dave Gannaway is in his fifth year as an assistant executive director of the IHSA with responsibility for officials. He was a coach and athletic director for many years before that and is the architect of the system for rating officials that has drawn so much attention in the state. Gannaway presented his information at the NASO Summit during a special bonus session.

The coach and official ratings combined are just one component of six that contribute to an official's "power rating" and are intended to allow objective comparison of officials in the IHSA's major sports. The power rating itself is a major element considered when determining playoff assignments.

The six components of the power rating are each worth up to five points for a maximum score of 30. Besides the coaches' and officials' ratings, the other five components are promotional level (Illinois recognizes three certification levels: registered, recognized and certified), NFHS exam score, previous tournament experience, number of varsity games worked and appearances on various "Top 15" lists (more on that later).

Part of the problem was that many officials took to the rating process cautiously. They wanted to trust the system but saw too much potential conflict of interest affecting their chances of receiving plum playoff assignments — even though only five of 30 power rating points were at stake.

Matters came to a head partway through the 2002-03 basketball season when Gannaway was informed that some officials were rating other officials a one when they had never seen those officials work. The rumored rationale was that enough such ballot box stuffing could help raise a power rating a point or two, perhaps making the difference between an assignment deep into the playoffs and not getting one at all.

"We received a letter from an official who said he had been encouraged (by his local association) to rate their member officials and rate them a one, even though he hadn't seen them work," says Gannaway.

That perceived corruption of the rating system didn't sit well with Gannaway and directly led to his investigation. The IHSA

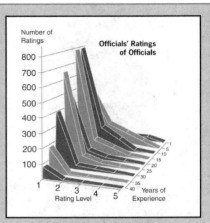

These charts show the number of each rating (1-5) that officials received listed by their years of experience. For example, officials with 40 years of experience received relatively few ratings of any number because there are relatively few officials who have 40 years of experience.

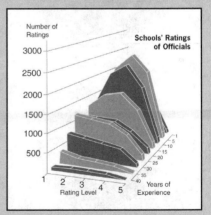

The charts show how skewed the ratings officials gave other officials were. Nearly everyone at all levels of experience received a rating of one or two. When schools rated officials, the larger number of ratings moved closer to the center of the chart, in the two, three and four range.

suspended the officials-rating-officials part of the online system and Gannaway undertook a statistical analysis of the submitted

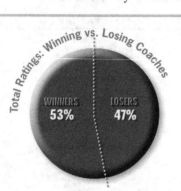

Of all the ratings submitted by schools during the 2002-03 season, a little more than half were from winning coaches.

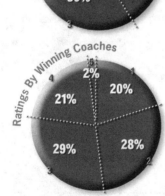

There was relatively little difference between losing coaches and winning coaches when it came to handing out the ratings. Winning coaches gave a one rating four percent more often than losing coaches, and losing coaches gave a five rating one percent more often than winning coaches. The two, three and four ratings remained remarkably similar.

ratings. That was in part to determine the extent of any wrongdoing and in part to address the standing concerns, mostly of officials, about the ability of coaches to rate them fairly.

Gannaway studied ratings data for the three complete years since they began in 2000-01. He determined the total number of ratings at each level for officials broken out over their number of years of experience. He segregated the data by comparing schools' ratings to officials' ratings. The resulting pattern is charted in the accompanying graphs (p. 79), using data from every fifth year of officials' experience for clarity.

It would appear that the schools' ratings of officials with increasing experience more closely followed the "bell curve" distribution one might expect, while the officials' ratings were skewed toward the superior.

Gannaway took a very close look at coaches during his analysis. When he looked at whether coaches are extracting a form of revenge by rating officials lower when they lose — a common perception among officials — the results said "no" again. When coaches send in their officials ratings, they designate whether they won or lost so it was easy to obtain the data: In 2002-03, of the 160,000-odd ratings submitted in which the sport had a winner and a loser, winning coaches gave officials a 2.56 rating on average against 2.75 for losing coaches. A little under 53 percent of all the ratings were from winning coaches. The distributions of the ratings are very similar, too, and seem to quell the case for retribution courtesy of the losing coaches.

Gannaway says, "I had no clue how coaches would rate depending on whether they won or lost. When you look at three years in a row, you now see that there's no real difference. Does it mean that a losing coach is not going to jab an official from time to time? In the big picture, they don't.

"We are only as good as the information that's on the computer," says Gannaway. "Is it giving us a pretty reliable sorting factor? Yes it is. It helps us get the information to put the right official in the right area."

The Impact of Media on Officiating

The question of officials' interaction with members of the media was debated during the NASO Summit session titled "Hanging Them Out to Dry." The crux of the debate was not the fact that officials will occasionally make mistakes and media people will often report on those mistakes. It had to do with how or even if the officials themselves should be allowed to comment on those mistakes to the media.

Crisis communication expert and amateur hockey official Dr. Francis J. Marra argued that officials should indeed be allowed to communicate with the media.

Marra developed a list of four recommendations that professional leagues can adopt to protect the hard-earned reputations of their officials. The ideas, he said, are based on well-accepted communication practices of successful businesses. The disadvantages are few. The benefits are many.

1. **Leagues should no longer tolerate unfair criticism of their officials.** The game officials are often the best in their profession. Commissioners and directors of officiating who accept unfair criticism as "part of the game" need to realize that "the game" has changed.

2. **Leagues must encourage officials to immediately explain controversial decisions.** Commissioners and directors of officiating need to recognize that officials will occasionally be the center of attention. Sequestering officials following a game only encourages additional negative publicity. A more effective strategy is to acknowledge the high-profile situation and allow the game officials to explain their decisions to reporters.

3. **Officials must accept the responsibilities that come with being public figures.** The intense coverage of professional sports has forever removed the anonymity of referees. Professional sports officials are now public figures and recognizable to many fans. Their names are widely known and bantered about casually on radio shows all over the country.

4. **Leagues should develop opportunities to showcase their officials away from games.** The many well-known officials in each league should take a leadership role and speak to community groups, youth associations or team fan clubs. They could also host live Internet chats to help educate amateur officials and fans about rules and how they are applied.

"It amazes me that an official at the professional level or Division I level can officiate a game in front of 100,000 people in a stadium, millions more on television, in the case of the National Football League they have the microphones, and yet they have the gag rule to prevent them from talking to reporters," said Marra. "The officials are very well-spoken, in most cases they're very intelligent people. Very quick one or two-day media training can teach them what they need to say, what they need to know, and what they don't need to know."

Other members of the panel disagreed with Marra's assertion that gag rules on officials should be lifted. The issue for Dr.

Ralph Swearngin, executive director of the Georgia High School Association and longtime amateur official himself, involved trusting the media.

"While I support Dr. Marra's research in theory, let me tell you where I live," Swearngin began. "I direct an association with 390 schools who are voluntary members, and we have about 6,500 to 7,000 of some of the greatest officials spread throughout our state who work with us. Georgia's an unusual state with a variety of some urban areas and a lot of rural areas. I'm not convinced that the *East Podunk Weekly Clarion,* whose staff is made up of alumni from East Podunk High School, when they feel like they got shafted by the official's call against West Podunk, really want a statement of fact from the officials. We've heard the old saying the pen is mightier than the sword. Let me tell you what's mightier than the pen, and that's the editor's scissors. Have you ever been interviewed for 20 or 30 minutes and they select a sentence from here and a sentence from here and they put them together, and the context is totally different than what you talked about? I get scared to death to think that our 6,500 to 7,000 officials might be called on right after a ballgame to articulate why they made a call when I'm not convinced the people asking the question really care a flip about that call as much as they want to find out what will make the readers' juices flow."

Lamell McMorris, spokesperson for the National Basketball Referees' Association, took another stand on the issue. "For those of us who have a unique perspective of representing or speaking on behalf of those who cannot speak to the media, it's not about whether I like or dislike the media," he said. "My challenge is to effectively use the media on behalf of the NBA referees (who otherwise are under a gag rule about speaking to the press).

Taking the hardest line on the opposite end of the spectrum from Marra's position was NFL Director of Officiating Mike Pereira. "If I'd give a young official some advice, I'd say keep your mouth shut (when dealing with the media). That's the way I am; I'm on the other end of (Marra). It's more important to deal with the administrators and how the administrators handle the conflict, and how they can get involved."

Background Checks

NCAA officials working championship events are subject to a background check. Professional leagues conduct extensive searches and many college conferences are now implementing some form of background review before hiring officials. Youth leagues are becoming more aggressive in requesting personal information on volunteers and officials?

But is there any consistent policy? What is acceptable and what crosses the line with respect to personal privacy?

Has a formal policy been established? Is there anyone out there looking at the long-term consequences?

Officials are sometimes referred to as a "necessary evil" by coaches and players. For officials, a "necessary evil" may be on the horizon in the form of a requirement for formal background checks in order to work.

Years ago, a certain junior senator from Wisconsin liked to ask, on nationwide television, "Are you now or have you ever been a member of the Communist party?" People lost their livelihood and careers for saying, "None of your business." It was almost worse than saying yes. What's the difference with all the variants of the background question — such as, "Have you ever been convicted of a felony?" — asked of officials? Is that a form of McCarthyism? Jack Roberts, executive director of the Michigan High School Athletic Association, said his organization automatically follows up on those people who leave the answer to the question blank. Indeed, Rick Wulkow, assistant executive director for the Iowa High School Athletic Association (IHSAA) is concerned that the can of worms opened by asking a background question would feed a large family of robins. The IHSAA, in fact, is evaluating starting to perform background checks and is currently looking for some legal advice on what collateral liability asking the questions poses.

"We want to have a sound reason for what we do and how we do it," Wulkow begins. "We're more on the issue of, 'Do we need to do this?'" The biggest issue I've run into, talking with legal people, is what effect does this have on your independent contractor status? In essence, once you ask these independent contractors this question, do they become your employees somehow and then you become liable for their conduct later?" Other than in most professional leagues or situations where officials are contracted out to leagues by an agent, your typical sports official is an independent contractor. An independent contractor is responsible for his or her own upkeep and simply provides a service in return for a fee. The significance of the term is that, in theory, the parent organization isn't liable for any negligence on the part of the official.

Alan Goldberger, a New Jersey lawyer specializing in the law as it applies to officials who moderated the NASO Summit panel on background checks, said the IHSAA's question isn't to be taken lightly. "Be careful what you wish for," he cautions. "The problem you run into is you need to be careful what you ask because you may find out more things than you want to know or need to know. And that opens you up to more decisions about that person than you might have banked on."

Goldberger describes the relationship between an official and his governing association as being somewhere on a continuum. "On the one end of this continuum you have an employer that hires officials and sends them out to leagues who need them — it's like outsourcing. In that case the officials are like employees and you'd better know their background. At the other end, it's like if you get a medical degree and then leave a sponge in the patient — nobody sues the medical school.

"Officials are somewhere in the middle," he explains. "The only thing you need to be careful about is that the closer you get to being an employer, the more obligations you have. From a school association's point of view then, it may be better to let officials associations conduct checks themselves from the point of view of management risk."

Goldberger adds that there is an important distinction in the official-association relationship that must be made in a case-by-

Why We Need Background Checks

By Brad Garrett, Oregon School Activities Association assistant executive director

Bob is a veteran basketball official with more than 20 years of oncourt experience. He is respected by many administrators, coaches and players on the court and off and has worked quite a few state championship events for the Oregon School Activities Association (OSAA) in several sports. Bob does not officiate in Oregon anymore.

Bob decided to pick up some extra money by serving as a swimming instructor for a pool during the morning hours. One afternoon after returning from a session there was a knock at his door and a sheriff was standing on his porch. It seems a student had reported to the sheriff's department that Bob tried to entice her to engage in some type of inappropriate behavior after a swimming lesson the previous day. Bob took the sheriff's recommendation and called an attorney.

The attorney advised Bob that the easiest way to clear up the situation was to take the plea bargain that would be offered. With no criminal convictions on his record the judge would most likely give him probation for a short period of time. Bob would not be subject to a lengthy court case and avoid becoming a poster boy for sexual abuse criminals.

Bob took the plea, Sexual Abuse IV, and settled for two years of probation. That is where the problems started for him. The OSAA requires that every official, as a condition of certification, takes and passes a criminal history conviction check. I don't know if Bob was innocent or guilty of the accusations made against him, but he pleaded guilty.

The issue of background checks is complicated but, in Oregon, we feel they are necessary. A defined set of parameters helps the OSAA staff determine which convictions merit non-certification. Essentially, if an official could obtain a teaching license in Oregon then he or she is allowed to officiate high school contests with some exceptions. The OSAA also keeps a record of those individuals who will never have the opportunity to represent any association in Oregon as an official. Most likely, those officials have engaged in felony behavior that involved a minor or other person, or have been incarcerated in a state or federal prison for an offense.

case basis. A few states actually "license" officials while the other organizations practice some form of "certification" of officials. He says that if a license is being granted there is a more formal definition of its effect and, "... it implies that a government is granting permission to a professional to do

According to an NFHS survey last year, only seven (Arizona, Idaho, Illinois, Kentucky, New Mexico, Oregon and Washington) of the 38 responding states require any type of formal background checks on officials. That is a remarkable statistic considering that last time I checked, crime happens in all states. If officials associations in other parts of the country are reflective of the Oregon numbers then somewhere between five and 10 percent of the officials seeking certification will have some type of criminal history that would merit a second look prior to placing them in situations in which they interact with middle or high school age children for any period of time.

Let's face it, sports officiating in this country is at a critical point. Local associations are out to recruit any potential new member that can demonstrate the ability to show up to assigned contests and handle the pressures associated with wearing the uniform. The bottom line is that games must be covered, and in many minds a conviction for something that happened in 1994 should not be a factor in determining whether you can call balls and strikes or determine a block from a charge.

That might be true if officiating was simply an assembly line activity without human interaction. Referees and umpires should be better than that. In Oregon character *does* make a difference. In this state, you will be held accountable for past mistakes because you represent the OSAA and the 287 member schools each time you put on the uniform adorned by the OSAA logo. The decision to conduct background checks is in the best interest of the schools we serve and the 115 local associations that represent the 3,300 officials in Oregon.

Everyone makes mistakes during a lifetime. Some will learn from experiences and move forward. Others forget the past much too quickly, making the same mistakes again and again.

As for Bob, he failed to pass the criminal conviction history check last year. I'm sure he would have chosen a different way to end an outstanding officiating career. In our last conversation, he had his hopes up because he had just finished packing up his house. He was moving to the Midwest for a new start in life and officiating.

something. If that's the case, then the states have wide discretion to extract information from whoever works for them." That kind of licensing is uncommon because sport organizations have typically made a point of constructing themselves as independent organizations from government and thus lost the ability to license. In comparison, he says, a certification is a less formal term and constitutes a permission to act as an official. When that's the case, "I don't think that you need to be concerned with being determined to be an employer of officials," says Goldberger. So does that mean, if it's all the same to the state, that an official applying for "certification" is free to decline to submit to the background check?

Not really. "There is nothing legally unsound for an organization to ask whether a person is of good moral character," Goldberger believes. "The general proposition is that it's legally sound to investigate and determine the applicant's character ... the official has to beyond reproach and impartial. He might be incompetent but that has nothing to do with whether he was dishonest. Some groups even require references and that's a good thing. There's nothing unenforceable about getting a lot of information on people."

Suppose you investigate a person and it's revealed, for example, that that person is an illegal alien. "Yeah, and what if a red herring jumps into my fishing boat?" you might scoff. Happens all the time, says Julie Ilacqua of the United States Soccer Federation. At the NASO Summit she said that her organization has problems like that because the soccer community is still highly immigrant based. Basically, suppose you run a background check and discover that the person doesn't exist? The organization gets put in the position of playing policeman whether it asked to or not.

Get used to the idea that the organization can ask the question and then can decline your services if it either doesn't get an answer or doesn't like the one it gets.

APPENDIX – I

"OFFICIALS AND SPORTSMANSHIP"
SURVEY

In June 2004, NASO conducted an Internet survey of those members who are subscribers to *LockerRoom*, NASO's monthly e-newsletter. Over 600 responded at the time survey results were compiled. The first 550 were used in determining the results. (Given that sample size, if we repeated the survey 100 times, we would expect the answer to any question to vary less than +/-4.0% in 95 of the 100 cases.) The questions were keyed to the topics that are to be discussed at "Sports Officiating 2004," NASO's annual conference. The intent of the survey was to obtain officials' views concerning the various issues that surface in discussion of: sportsmanship, background checks, security, media relations and continuing officiating education. The survey results follow:

1. What sports do you officiate?
41% Baseball
43% Basketball
39% Football
2% Ice Hockey
13% Soccer
27% Softball
1% Swimming
2% Track and Field
9% Volleyball
1% Wrestling
9% Other(s)

2. What is the primary level of games you work?
4% Rec league
6% Youth
1% Freshman
5% Junior varsity
61% High school varsity
13% Small college
7% Major college
1% Professional
2% Other

3. How long have you been officiating?
1% Less than one year
10% 1-4 years
17% 5-9 years
19% 10-14 years
14% 15-19 years
39% 20 or more years

4. Of these professional sports, which demonstrates the poorest sportsmanship?
7% Baseball
47% Basketball
11% Football
29% Ice Hockey
6% Soccer

5. Of these professional sports, which demonstrates the best sportsmanship?
39% Baseball
6% Basketball
24% Football
9% Ice Hockey
22% Soccer

6. Sportsmanship is worst at what level?
30% Rec league
20% Youth
 9% High school
 3% College
38% Pro

7. Sportsmanship is best at what level?
 6% Rec league
25% Youth
34% High school
32% College
 3% Pro

8. What effect do acts of poor sportsmanship at the higher levels of sport have on sportsmanship at the lower levels?
77% A huge effect
22% Some effect
 1% Just a little effect
 0% No effect

9. At the primary level you work, what has been the sportsmanship trend over the past five years? Sportsmanship has: (*choose only one*)
 5% Not applicable, I have worked less than five years
17% Gotten a lot worse
32% Gotten slightly worse
28% Stayed about the same
18% Slightly improved
 5% Improved a lot

10. Which group of people has the most responsibility for improving sportsmanship?
14% Players
64% Coaches
 2% Officials
15% Administrators
 5% Fans
 1% Media

11. Which group of people is best positioned to have the greatest impact on sportsmanship?
12% Players
65% Coaches
 5% Officials
10% Administrators
 2% Fans
 6% Media

12. Do leaders of organized sports at all levels have a common vision for improving sportsmanship in our games?
24% Yes
76% No

13. Do you agree with this statement: "Poor sportsmanship is the number-one problem in our games today"?
76% Yes
24% No

14. Are the rules in your primary sport clear on defining what constitutes an unsportsmanlike act?
79% Yes
21% No

15. Do you believe that officials rule on poor sportsmanship differently when it is a "big game" or playoff/championship game?
77% Yes
23% No

16. Do you believe that officials and their associations do enough to help improve sportsmanship?
35% Yes
65% No

17. Which of these statements best reflects your belief concerning officials and sportsmanship? (*choose one*)
 5% Officials are responsible for establishing an atmosphere of good sportsmanship in a game.
89% Officials are partners with players, coaches and administrators in establishing an atmosphere of good sportsmanship in a game.
 6% Officials are enforcers. They are there to note and penalize unsportsmanlike acts.

18. Are you satisfied with the level of support you get from your assigners and/or league authorities when you penalize acts of poor sportsmanship?
78% Yes
22% No

19. At the primary level you work, do sports officials have the tools (training, authority, knowledge, courage) to make a significant impact on improving sportsmanship?
54% Yes
46% No

20. At the primary level you work, what tool do officials most lack when it comes to making a significant impact on improving sportsmanship?
20% Training
14% Authority
7% Knowledge
46% Courage
13% None of the above

21. Other than physical or health reasons what do you believe is the main reason people stop officiating? (*choose one*)
3% Low pay
1% Inadequate training
17% Time pressures
11% Too difficult to advance
44% Problems with coaches/players/fans
14% Burnout
1% Concern for their safety
8% It's not what they expected
1% Other

22. Should officials be required to undergo background checks as a prerequisite to officiating at high school and lower levels?
70% Yes
30% No

23. Should officials be required to undergo background checks as a prerequisite to officiating at college and higher levels?
70% Yes
30% No

24. How do you view your personal safety concerns as an official compared to five years ago? (*choose only one*)
7% Not applicable, I have worked less than five years
12% I am much more concerned
31% I am slightly more concerned
44% I am concerned about the same
5% I am concerned somewhat less
1% I am concerned much less

25. At the primary level you work, are you satisfied with what game administrators have done to ensure your physical safety?
60% Yes
40% No

26. Have you been assaulted as a result of a game in which you have worked?
19% Yes
81% No

27. During the last year were you ever concerned about your physical safety because of a game situation?
30% Yes
70% No

28. As a general rule, do you believe officiating errors should be made public after the game is over?
9% Yes, all the time
55% Sometimes
36% Never

29. Should officials be authorized to meet with members of the media in postgame sessions to discuss game situations?
15% Yes
57% No
28% Maybe

30. Do you believe that some form of continuing education for veteran officials should be required?
91% Yes
2% No
7% Maybe

31. If there was a requirement for continuing education for veteran officials how would you prefer that the education program be delivered? (*choose one*)

48% Through my local officials association in a classroom setting
35% On a regional basis by a state or other authority in a classroom setting
16% On an individual basis through the Internet
1% On an individual basis through the mail

APPENDIX – II

NASO Sports Officiating Summit 2004 Session List

YOU DON'T HAVE TO BE SICK TO GET BETTER — That's the title of the book authored by our keynoter, Michael Josephson. Josephson's the founder and president of the Josephson Institute of Ethics, which helps people make principled decisions and live with greater integrity. The CHARACTER COUNTS! Coalition, inspired by Josephson, is a widespread partnership of schools and youth-serving organizations. He launched the "Pursuing Victory With Honor" sportsmanship campaign that is endorsed by virtually all amateur organizations.

SPORTSMANSHIP: VIEW FROM THE TOP — What are the root causes of poor sportsmanship? How can what is acceptable behavior at one level be totally unacceptable at other levels? Do the leaders of organized sports have a common vision for improving sportsmanship in our games? Does "simply enforce the rules" work for officials? Barry Mano, NASO president and *Referee* magazine publisher, looked for answers as the moderator of a star-studded panel that included: Bob Kanaby, NFHS executive director; Jon Butler, Pop Warner Football executive director; and Dennis Poppe, NCAA managing director of baseball and football.

WHAT'S THE OFFICIAL'S ROLE? — We bore down on defining the role of the official in improving sportsmanship. Is it as simple as standing back and taking names — being solely the enforcer — or can officials take positive actions that in turn will result in an environment that will encourage improvements in sportsmanship? Bill Topp, *Referee* magazine editor, revealed the results of an NASO-member survey of the official's proper role in sportsmanship and seeks to build a consensus among Summit participants.

FINDING TAKE-CHARGE SOLUTIONS — Leading off this session, Gary Whelchel, Arizona Interscholastic Association commissioner of officials, described his state's experience with the "Pursuing Victory With Honor" program. Gary supplied hard data that showed progress in the effort to improve sportsmanship. Following that, attendees divided up into small groups to brainstorm independent actions that should be considered by officials and their associations to stake out a leadership position in sportsmanship.

CASE STUDY: REFS RATING REFS — Dave Gannaway, assistant executive director of the Illinois High School Association, reported on the IHSA's experience with ratings of officials by coaches and fellow officials. Dave charted and analyzed a season's worth of data. Everybody knows you just can't trust coaches to rate officials, right? What about refs rating refs? The results were surprising.

BACKGROUND CHECKS: EVIL OR NECESSARY? — Inexorable forces seem to be making background checks more of an inevitability in the future of officials. What has been the experience to date? What are the legal and practical issues involved? What must leaders be aware of? Alan Goldberger, sports law attorney and recognized legal authority on officiating law, moderated a panel that included: U.S. District Court Judge Jack Bissell; Brad Garrett, Oregon School Activities Association assistant executive director; Marc Ratner, executive director of boxing's Nevada State Athletic Commission and high school commissioner of officials in Southern Nevada; and Julie Ilacqua, managing director of federation services at the U.S. Soccer Federation.

OFFICIATING ON TAP — This was a free-flowing, happy hour setting event and attendees selected the topic of conversation. Each of a dozen or so tables featured a different topic. Topics and facilitators included: legal/independent contractor issues (Alan Goldberger, sports law attorney), identification of quality officials (Marcy Weston, NCAA national coordinator of women's basketball officiating), insurance protection, assigning (Marc Ratner, high school commissioner of officials in Southern Nevada), training (Jerry Seeman, former NFL senior director of officiating), finances/fundraising, diversity in recruiting (Anita Ortega, major college women's basketball official), cyberspace development (Maltbie Brown, local association officer; Reid Evans, president of Advanced Business Technologies), background checks (Julie Ilacqua, USSF managing director of federation services).

BE CAREFUL OUT THERE — A secure game environment has worked its way up the officiating priority list. Not that it wasn't important in the past, just that it wasn't as difficult to achieve. Current newspaper headlines stand witness to safety and personal security issues that do damage to our games and shorten officiating careers. Dave Yeast, NCAA national coordinator of umpires, lead a discussion of those challenges with Ronnie Carter, Tennessee Secondary School Athletic Association executive director; Anita Ortega, 20-year veteran of the Los Angeles Police Department and major college women's basketball referee; Milt Ahlerich, NFL vice-president for security; and Kathy Spangler, National Recreation and Park Association national partnerships director.

HANGING THEM OUT TO DRY — Officiating calls at every level have never been more highly scrutinized. Errors are made, sure, but what is gained by a public announcement of specific mistakes. What errors should be announced? How and when? What constitutes a punishable offense? Any chance that good performance will be acknowledged? Panelists: Mike Pereira, NFL director of officiating; Ralph Swearngin, Georgia High School Association executive director; and representation from the media and for NBA officials, sorted out those challenges with Tom Herre, Referee Enterprises VP, as moderator.

FOURTH DOOOOOOWN! — Legendary retired NFL referee Red Cashion had the last word. Red underscored the critical part officials play in our games. His down home humor, savvy advice and stout performance across a long career have made him an icon in the sports world.

APPENDIX – III

NASO Sports Officiating Summit 2004
Speaker List

Milt Ahlerich — NFL vice president of security with responsibility for all security programs including player and employee conduct issues; formerly worked for the FBI, where he held three of the Bureau's 10 most senior executive positions.

Marcia Alterman — Professional Association of Volleyball Officials executive director and former president; named as the first NCAA women's volleyball rules interpreter in 2002; numerous postseason assignments at all levels of collegiate volleyball; Big 10 Conference and Conference USA coordinator of volleyball officials; Officiating Development Alliance member.

Esse Baharmast — USSF director of advancement and international referee development; former USSF director of officials; retired international referee; worked two 1998 World Cup games in France; became the first American referee to whistle two World Cup matches; recipient of 1997 MLS Referee of the Year Award; worked 1996 Olympic games; NASO Board member.

Judge Jack Bissell — Chief Judge, U.S. District Court District of N.J.; retired high school and small college ice hockey official.

Paul Brazeau — NBA director of basketball operations/officiating performance analysis; responsible for monitoring the daily performance of NBA referees; oversees a staff of observers who critique the performances of the officials in person and review all referees calls on video tape.

Malt Brown — Current high school basketball and football official; Central Ohio District Officials Committee president and Central Ohio Basketball Officials Association secretary and treasurer.

Jon Butler — Pop Warner Little Scholars executive director; former president of a company that manufactured football blocking sleds and field equipment; former high school assistant football coach; former National Council of Youth Sports director; serves as board member for Touchdown Club of America, Philadelphia Sports Congress and USA Football.

Anthony "Corky" Carter — Semi-pro, college and high school softball and high school baseball umpire; former college umpire evaluator and Houston USSSA Umpires Association president; worked a total of four softball World Series including one men's and women's USSSA and two men's NSA series; inducted into the Texas USSSA Hall of Fame in 1997.

Ronnie Carter — Tennessee Secondary School Athletic Association executive director; former high school teacher, coach, official and administrator; served on many committees, including the NFHS football rules, NFHS basketball and wrestling rules committees; immediate past president of the NFHS board of directors; NASO Board member.

Red Cashion — Retired in 1997 as an NFL referee; worked Super Bowls XX and XXX; worked 18 playoff games and Pro Bowl; currently serves as trainer for NFL referees; Professional Football Referees Association past president; inducted into the Texas Sports Hall of Fame in 1999; former NASO Board treasurer.

Randy Christal — Major college football and baseball official; worked NCAA Division I-A football national championships in 1997 and 2003; eight NCAA Division I baseball College World Series and the 1984 summer Olympics; NASO Board chair.

Danny Crawford — NBA referee; worked games in the last eight Finals; previously worked in the Continental Basketball Association; former high school baseball umpire; NASO Board member.

Craig Cress — Amateur Softball Association director of membership services; worked 10 ASA fast pitch national championships, two world competitions and two international events; serves as a clinician at ASA national umpires schools and umpire-in-chief for several national championships.

Don Cronin — Former *USA Today* assignment editor and Mid-Atlantic sports editor for United Press International; high school and small college basketball official; worked 14 public school and eight private school state tournaments and the Capital Athletic Conference championship game.

Reid Evans — Advanced Business Technology president and founder. Creator of The Arbiter assigning software program; NASO Education Partner.

Ron Foxcroft — Fox 40 International chairman and founder; former major college and international men's basketball official; worked 1976 Olympic Gold Medal Championship basketball game; NBA officials observer; inducted into six halls of fame; NASO Foundation trustee; NASO Board special adviser; NASO Education Partner; former ODA member.

Dave Gannaway — Illinois High School Association assistant executive director with primary areas of responsibility for football, wrestling, softball and officials; named Illinois Wrestling Coaches and Officials Association Administrator of the Year in 1992; winner of the Illinois State Award of Merit for the National Interscholastic Athletic Administrators Association.

Brad Garrett — Oregon School Activities Association assistant executive director; staff liaison to the Oregon Athletic Officials Association and certifies officials in all local associations within Oregon; NFHS wrestling rules committee member; served on the Oregon Athletic Directors Association and NIAAA Leadership Training National Faculty committees.

Alan Goldberger — Sports law attorney and recognized legal authority for game officials; author of *Sports Officiating: A Legal Guide*; frequent speaker to groups of game officials, coaches, recreation professionals and attorneys; member, counsel and chair of many officials associations; former baseball and football official; worked men's and women's major college basketball; Referee contributor.

Julie Ilacqua — USSF managing director of Federation services; oversees the recruitment, training and development of referees from youth to professional and international matches; former National Referee Committee chair; former NASO Board member and chair; Officiating Development Alliance member.

Michael Josephson — Josephson Institute of Ethics founder and president; founder of Character Counts!, the nation's leading character education system; launched the Pursuing Victory With Honor sportsmanship campaign, which is endorsed by virtually all amateur athletic organizations; NASO Board member-elect.

Bob Kanaby — NFHS executive director; former New Jersey State Interscholastic Activities Athletic Association (NJSIAA) executive director; leader in the organization and alliance of the Citizenship Through Sports and Fine Arts Curriculum; serves on the USA Basketball and Naismith Basketball Hall of Fame board of directors.

Tom Lepperd — Major League Baseball director of umpire administration; former minor league umpire; AL regular season fill-in from 1984-86; member of Umpire Development Program; former NL assistant director of umpires; Officiating Development Alliance member.

Barry Mano — NASO founder and president; Referee Enterprises, Inc. founder and president; publisher of *Referee* magazine; NASO Foundation trustee; former major college basketball official; Officiating Development Alliance member; NASO Board president.

Frank Marra — Public relations and crisis management expert. Applies his experience to enhance and protect the reputation of sports officials; one of the few people in the world to have a doctoral degree specifically in public relations; regularly teaches a full-semester course in crisis management; 30-year amateur sports official.

Lamell McMorris — Perennial Strategy Group (PSG) founder and principal, PSG represents the NBA officials; works in the public and private sector to transform his insight and energy into the establishment of the PSG consulting firm; Southern Christian Leadership Conference executive director and chief operating officer; obtained a masters degree in ethics and public policy.

Anita Ortega — Los Angeles Police Department commanding officer; major college women's basketball official; inducted into the UCLA Athletic Hall of Fame and worked the Pac-10 women's basketball tournament in 2002; worked eight consecutive NCAA women's basketball tournaments; worked the 1978 UCLA women's basketball championship; NASO Board member.

Mike Pereira — NFL director of officiating; former NFL supervisor and Western Athletic Conference supervisor of officials; retired NFL and major college football official; worked eight college bowl games; Officiating Development Alliance member.

Dennis Poppe — NCAA managing director for baseball and football with direct responsibility for the administration of baseball and football championships and coordination of playing rules; serves as the primary liaison to the NCAA Division I Baseball Committee, NCAA Baseball Rules Committee, American Baseball Coaches Association and USA Baseball; College World Series tournament director.

Joan Powell — Professional Association of Volleyball Officials president; longtime high school teacher, coach and volleyball official; five-time NCAA Division I Final Four referee; NASO Board secretary.

Marc Ratner — Nevada State Athletic Commission executive director; Southern District of Nevada for High School Athletics commissioner; Southern Nevada commissioner of officials; major college football official; NASO Board treasurer.

Stephen Rey — University of Southern Mississippi recreational sports associate director; National Intramural Recreational Sports Association (NIRSA) member and chair of the sports officials development program; National Collegiate Flag Football Championships director of officials; U.S. Army Europe sports program officials clinician; high school and small college football, basketball, women's basketball, and indoor professional football official; Amateur Softball Association tournament director and umpire; Officiating Development Alliance member.

Jerry Seeman — NFL consultant; former NFL senior director of officiating, NFL official and high school basketball official; worked two Super Bowls; past Officiating Development Alliance member and current NASO Board vice chair.

Larry Spann — Department of State and National Security Agency top secret background and security clearances investigator; formerly worked for the U.S. Courts, Department of Justice and various corporate entities.

Jeff Stern — Referee Enterprises, Inc. senior editor with specific responsibility for football and baseball coverage; high school and college football official; high school baseball umpire; former basketball, wrestling and softball official.

Mary Struckhoff — NFHS assistant director; NFHS basketball and softball rules interpreter and editor; NFHS Officials Association and Officials Education Program staff liaison; major college women's basketball and former volleyball official; former Illinois High School Association assistant executive director; Officiating Development Alliance member.

Ralph Swearngin — Georgia High School Association executive director and former commissioner of officials; high school football official; NFHS Football Rules Committee member and NFHS Softball Rules Committee Chair; multiple sport state interpreter.

Bill Topp — Referee magazine vice president of publishing and management services; high school and college basketball and high school football official; former major college baseball umpire and small college football official; 2000 NCAA Division III World Series umpire; Officiating Development Alliance member.

Marcy Weston — Central Michigan University senior associate athletic director and NCAA national coordinator of women's basketball officiating; worked 1982 and 1984 NCAA women's basketball championships; Women's Basketball Hall of Fame inductee; named in 1991 as one of nine major contributors to first decade of NCAA women's basketball; former NASO Board member and chair; Officiating Development Alliance member.

Gary Whelchel — Arizona Interscholastic Association commissioner of officials; NFHS Basketball Rules Committee member; basketball, volleyball and softball high school official; worked 24 consecutive state basketball tournaments, seven state basketball championship games and four state volleyball championship games; AIA State Officials Committee member; former NASO Board member

Dave Yeast — NCAA national coordinator of baseball umpires; Amateur Baseball Umpires Association board member; worked two College World Series and the 1996 Olympics; former Missouri Valley and Conference USA baseball supervisor of umpires; Officiating Development Alliance member.

Henry Zaborniak Jr. — Ohio High School Athletic Association assistant commissioner; current major college football official; former collegiate women's and men's basketball and retired NFL Europe official; NASO Board member.